Anonymous

Railroad Laws of New Mexico

Anonymous

Railroad Laws of New Mexico

ISBN/EAN: 9783744667180

Printed in Europe, USA, Canada, Australia, Japan

Cover: Foto ©Suzi / pixelio.de

More available books at **www.hansebooks.com**

OF

NEW MEXICO.

COMPILED BY

MESSRS. CATRON & THORNTON,

ATTORNEYS AT LAW,

SANTA FE, N. M.

SANTA FE:
New Mexican Book & Job Printing Department.
1881.

INDEX.

RAILROAD LAWS OF NEW MEXICO.

CHAPTER III.

AN ACT to create a general incorporation law, permitting persons to associate themselves together as bodies corporate for mining, manufacturing and other industrial pursuits.

Be it enacted by the Legislative Assembly of the Territory of New Mexico:

SECTION 1. Corporations for mining, manufacturing and other industrial pursuits, may be formed according to the provisions of this act, such corporations and members thereof being subject to all the conditions and liabilities herein imposed, and to none others.

SEC. 2. Any three or more persons, who may desire to form a company for any one or more of the purposes specified in the preceding section, may make, sign, and acknowledge before the Secretary of the Territory, or some officer competent to take the acknowledgment of deeds, and file in the office of the Secretary of the Territory a certificate in writing (for the filing of which said certificate the Secretary shall receive a fee of ten dollars) in which shall be set forth the full names of such persons, the corporate name of the company, the objects for which the company shall be formed, the amount of its capital stock, the time of its existence, not to exceed fifty years, the number of shares of which the stock shall consist, the number of directors and their names, who shall manage the concerns of the company for the first three months, and the name of the city or town and county in which the principal place of business of the company is located. A copy of said certificate, duly certified by the Secretary of the Territory, shall be filed in the office of the Probate Clerk of the county where the principal place of business of the corporation is located. The

Secretary of the Territory upon the payment of the fees authorized by law shall furnish any person interested as many certified copies as may be required

SEC. 3. A copy of any certificate of incorporation filed in pursuance of this act, and certified by the Secretary of the Territory shall be received in all the courts and places as presumptive evidence of the facts therein.

SEC. 4. When the certificate shall have been filed, the persons who shall have signed and acknowledged the same, their associates and successors, shall be a body politic and corporate in fact and in name, by the name stated in the certificate and by their corporate name have succession for the period limited; and power: 1st. To sue and be sued in any court; 2d. To make and use a common seal, and alter the same at pleasure; 3d. To purchase, hold, sell, mortgage and convey real and personal estate as the purposes of the corporation shall require; 4th. To appoint such officers, agents and servants, as the business of the corporation shall require, to define their power, prescribe their duties and fix their compensation; 5th. To require of them such security as may be thought proper for the fulfilment of their duties, and to remove them at will, except that no director shall be removed from office unless by a vote of two-thirds of the whole number of directors; 6th. To make by-laws not inconsistent with the laws of this Territory, for the organization of the company, the management of its property, the regulation of its affairs, the transfer of its stock, and for carrying on all kinds of business within the objects and purposes of the company.

SEC. 5. The corporate powers of the corporation shall be exercised by a board of not less than three directors, who shall be stockholders in the company and a majority of them citizens of the United States and residents of this Territory, and who shall, after the expiration of the term of the directors first selected, be annually elected by the stockholders, at such time and place, and upon such notice, and in such mode, as shall be directed by the by-laws of the company: but all elections shall be by ballot, and each stockholder, either in person or by proxy, shall be entitled to as many votes as he owns shares of stock, and the persons receiving the greatest number of votes shall be directors. When any vacancy shall happen among the directors by death, resignation or otherwise, it shall be filled, for the remainder of the year, in such manner as may be provided by the by-laws of the company.

SEC. 6. If it should happen, at any time, that an election of directors shall not be made on the day designated by the by-laws of the company, the corporation shall not for that reason be dissolved, but it shall be lawful on any other day to hold an election for directors in such manner as shall be provided for by the by-laws of the company; and all acts of directors shall be valid and binding upon the company until their successors shall be elected.

SEC. 7. A majority of the whole number of directors shall form a board for the transaction of business, and every decision of a majority of the persons duly assembled as a board, shall be valid as a corporate act.

SEC. 8. The first meeting of the directors shall be called by a notice signed by one or more of the persons named directors in the certificate, setting forth the time and place of the meeting, which notice shall be either delivered personally to each director, or published at least ten days in some newspaper of the county in which is the principal place of business of the corporation, or if no newspaper be published in the county, then by posting up legible notices in six of the most public places in said county for the period before named.

SEC. 9 The stock of the company shall be deemed personal estate and shall be transferable in such manner as shall be prescribed by the by-laws of the company; but no transfer shall be valid, except between the parties thereto, until the same shall be so entered on the books of the company, as to show the names of the parties by and to whom transferred, the number and designation of the shares, and the date of the transfer.

SEC. 10. The directors shall have power to call in and demand from the stockholders the sums by them subscribed, at such times and in such payments or instalments as they may deem proper; notice of each assessment shall be given to the stockholders personally, or shall be published once a week, for at least four weeks, in some newspaper published at the place designated as the principal place of business of the corporation, or, if none be published there, then by posting such notice for that period in at least six of the most public places in the county in which said principal place of business of the corporation is located. If after such notice has been given, any stockholder shall make default in the payment of the assessment upon the shares held by him, so many of such shares may be sold as will be necessary for the payment of the assessment on all the shares held by him. The sale of said shares shall be made as prescribed in the by-laws of the company; provided, that no sales shall be made except at public auction to the highest bidder after a notice of thirty days published as above directed in this section;

and that at such sale the person who will agree to pay the assessment so due, together with the expenses of advertisement and other expenses of sale for the smallest number of whole shares, shall be deemed the highest bidder.

SEC. 11. Whenever any stock is held by any person as executor, administrator, or guardian or trustee, he shall represent such stock at all meetings of the company, and may vote accordingly as a stockholder.

SEC. 12. Any stockholder may pledge his stock by a delivery of the certificate or other evidence of his interest, but may nevertheless represent the same at all meetings, and vote accordingly as a stockholder.

SEC. 13. It shall not be lawful for the directors to make any dividend except from the surplus profits arising from the business of the corporation ; nor to divide, withdraw, or in any way pay to the stockholders, or any of them, any part of the capital stock of the company ; nor to reduce the capital stock unless in the manner prescribed in this act ; and in case of any violations of the provisions of this section, the directors under whose administration the same may have happened, except those who may have caused their dissent therefrom to be entered at large on the minutes of the board of directors at the time, or were not present when the same did happen, shall in their individual and private capacities be jointly and severally liable to the corporation, and the creditors thereof in the event of its dissolution, to the full amount so divided, withdrawn, paid out or reduced ; provided that this section shall not be construed to prevent a division and distribution of the capital stock of the company, which shall remain after the payment of all its debts, upon the dissolution of the corporation or the expiration of its charter.

SEC. 14. The total amount of debts of the corporation shall not at any time exceed the amount of the capital stock ; and in case of any excess, the directors under whose administration the same may have happened, except those who may have caused their dissent therefrom to be entered at large on the minutes of the board of directors at the time, and except those not present when the same did happen, shall, in their individual and private capacities, be liable jointly and severally, to the said corporation, and in the event of its dissolution, to any of the creditors thereof, for the full amount of such excess.

SEC. 15. No person holding stock as executor, guardian or trustee, or holding it as collateral security, or in pledge, shall be personally subject to any liability as a stockholder of the company ; but the person pledging the stock shall be considered as holding the same, and shall be liable as a stockholder accordingly; and the estate and funds in the hands of the executor, administrator, guardian or trustee, shall be liable in like manner, and to the same extent as the testator or intestate, or the ward or person interested in the trust fund would have been if he had been living and competent to act and hold the stock in his own name.

Sec. 16. It shall be the duty of the directors of every company incorporated under this act, for the purpose of ditching, mining, or conveying water for mining purposes, to cause a book to be kept containing the names of all persons, alphabetically arranged, who are or shall become stockholders of the corporation, and showing the number of designation of shares of stock held by them respectively, and the time when they respectively became the owners of such shares; also a book or books in which shall be entered at length, in a plain and simple manner, all by-laws, orders and resolutions of the company and board of directors, and the manner and time of their adoption, which books during the business hours of the day, Sundays and fourth of July excepted, shall be opened for the inspection of stockholders and the creditors of the company, each individual stockholder, and their duly authorized agents and attorneys, at the office or principal place of business of the company; provided, that the office and books of every such company shall be kept, and the books of the company shall be open as aforesaid, in the county in which their business is transacted; and every stockholder and creditor as aforesaid, or their agents or attorneys, shall have the right to make extracts from such books, or, upon payment of reasonable clerk's fees therefor, to demand and receive from the clerk or other officer having the charge of such books, a certified copy of any entry made therein; such book or certified copy of any entry shall be presumptive evidence of the facts therein stated, in any action or proceeding against the company or any one or more stockholders. Provided, that such provisions concerning water made by virtue of this law will not in any manner impede the rights or privileges of those who are employed in agriculture.

Sec. 17. Any company incorporated under this act may, by complying with the provisions herein contained, increase or diminish its capital stock to any amount which may be deemed sufficient and proper for the purposes of the corporation; but before any incorporation shall be entitled to diminish the amount of its capital stock, if the amount of its debts and liabilities shall exceed the sum to which the capital is proposed to be diminished, such amount shall be satisfied and reduced so as not to exceed the diminished amount of capital.

SEC. 18. Whenever it is desired to increase or diminish the amount of capital stock, a meeting of stockholders may be called, by a notice signed by at least a majority of directors, and published for at least four weeks as provided in section ten of this act, which notice shall specify the object of the meeting, the time and place where it is to be held, and the amount to which it is proposed to increase or diminish the capital, and a vote of two-thirds of all the shares of stock shall be necessary to increase or diminish the amount of capital stock.

SEC. 19. If at any meeting so called, a sufficient number of votes has been given in favor of increasing or diminishing the amount of capital, a certificate of the proceedings showing a compliance with these provisions, the amount of capital actually paid in, the whole amount of debts and liabilities of the company, and the amount to which the capital stock is to be increased or diminished, shall be made out, signed and verified by the affidavit of the chairman and secretary of the meeting, certified by a majority of the directors, and filed as required by the second section of this act, and when so filed the capital stock of the corporation shall be increased or diminished to the amount specified in the certificate.

SEC. 20. Upon the dissolution of any corporation formed under this act, the directors at the time of dissolution shall be directors of the creditors and stockholders of the corporation dissolved, and shall have full power and authority to sue for and recover the debts and property of the corporation by the name of directors of the corporation, collect and pay the outstanding debts, settle all its affairs, and divide amongst the stockholders the money and other property that shall remain after the payment of the debts and necessary expenses.

SEC. 21. Any corporation formed under this act may dissolve and disincorporate itself, by presenting to the probate judge of the county in which the meetings of the directors are usually held, a petition to that effect, accompanied by a certificate of its proper officers, and setting forth that at a general or special meeting of the stockholders called for that purpose, it was decided by a vote of two-thirds of all the stockholders, to disincorporate and dissolve the corporation; notice of the application shall then be given by the clerk, which notice shall set forth the nature of the application, and shall specify the time and place at which it is to be heard, and shall be published as provided in section ten of this act. At the time and place appointed, or at any other to which it may be postponed by the judge, he shall proceed to consider the application, and if satisfied that the corporation has taken the necessary preliminary steps, and obtained the necessary vote to dissolve itself, and that all claims against the corporation are discharged, he shall enter an order declaring it dissolved.

SEC. 22. If any corporation formed under this act, shall not organize and commence the transaction of its business within two years from the date of the filing the certificate of its incorporation, its corporate powers shall cease.

SEC. 23. That all corporations heretofore formed by virtue of any law of this territory, shall comply with and conform to the provisions of this act, so far as the same shall be applicable and shall not interfere with any vested right.

SEC. 24. That whenever any persons shall have formed themselves into an incorporation according to the provisions of this act, it shall not be lawful for any other persons to become incorporated under the same name or designation, nor for the same immediate purpose. This last provision shall not apply to mining, mechanical or manufacturing operations.

SEC. 25. That all acts and parts of acts in conflict with the provisions of this act are hereby repealed, and this act shall be in full force and effect from and after its passage and approval.

Approved December 27th, 1867.

CHAPTER XXXI.

AN ACT To amend an act entitled an act to create a general incorporation act permitting persons to associate themselves together as bodies corporate for mining, manufacturing and other industrial pursuits, and to repeal the sixteenth section of said act.

Be it enacted by the Legislative Assembly of the Territory of New Mexico:

SECTION 1. That an act entitled an act to create a general incorporation law permitting persons to associate themselves together as bodies corporate for mining, manufacturing and other industrial pursuits, approved the 28th day of December, 1867, be repealed in its sixteenth section and amended as follows :

SEC. 2. That any association of persons incorporated under the general incorporation law of any other contiguous state or territory of the United States for the purpose of constructing telegraph lines, railroads or wagon roads, desiring to extend the construction of such lines of telegraph, railroad or wagon roads into this Territory shall be required to register in the office of the Secretary of this Territory, and in the office of the clerk of the probate court of the county in which their principal business office may be established, the original or a certified copy of the articles of incorporation thus obtained from such contiguous state or territory.

SEC. 3. At the time of recording such articles of incorporation and association in the opinion [office?] of the Secretary as required in the foregoing section, such persons shall be entitled, for the purposes for which they were incorporated, to all the rights, benefits and privileges secured by the provisions of the act to which this is an amendment; provided, this association of persons shall be required to conform to all the provisions of the said act to which this is an amendment.

SEC. 4. That the Secretary of this Territory shall be entitled to receive for recording articles of association the same fees mentioned in the act to which this is an amendment.

SEC. 5. This act shall be in force from and after its passage.

Approved Jauuary 30, 1868.

[Translation.]

CHAPTER XIII.

AN ACT providing for mortgaging and consolidating lines of railway in this Territory.

Be it enacted by the Legislative Assembly of the Territory of New Mexico:

SECTION 1. That any railroad company heretofore or hereafter organized under the laws of this Territory, shall have power to borrow money and purchase property, real and personal, for the use of the corporation, and to mortgage and pledge all or any part of its corporate franchises and property in possession or subsequently to be acquired, as security for the payment of the money so borrowed and for the payment of the purchase money for the property so purchased.

SEC. 2. That any railroad company heretofore or hereafter organized under the laws of this Territory, may at any time by means of subscription to the capital of any other company or otherwise aid such company in the construction of its railroad within or without the Territory for the purpose of forming a connection with the said last mentioned road with the road owned by the company furnishing such aid, or any railroad organized in pursuance of law, either within this or any other territory or state, may lease or purchase any part or all of any railroad constructed, owned or leased by any other company upon such terms and conditions as may be agreed on between such companies respectively, or any two or more railroad companies may enter into any arrangement for their common benefit consistent with, and calculated to promote the objects for which they were created ; provided, that no such aid shall be furnished, nor any purchase, lease, subletting or arrangements perfected until a meeting of stockholders of such company of this Territory, party to such agreement, shall have been called by the directors thereof, at such time and place and in such manner as they shall designate, and the holders of at least two-thirds of the stock of such company represented at such meeting, in person or by proxy, and voting thereat, shall have assented thereto.

SEC. 3. It shall and may be lawful for any railroad company or corporation organized under the laws of this Territory, or of this territory and any other territory or state, and operating a railroad or bridge, either wholly within, or partly within and partly without this Territory, to merge and consolidate its capital stock, franchises and property with the capital stock, franchises and property of any other railroad company or companies organized under the laws of this Territory, or under the laws of this territory and any other territory or state, whenever the two or more railroads of the companies or corporations so to be consolidated shall or may form a continuous line of railroad with each other, or by means of any intervening railroad, bridge or ferry.

SEC. 4. Said consolidation shall be made under the conditions, provisions and restrictions, and with the powers hereinafter in this act mentioned and contained, that is to say :

First, the directors of the companies proposing to consolidate may enter into a joint agreement under the corporate seal of each company for the consolidation of said companies and railroads, and prescribing the terms and conditions thereof, the mode of carrying the same into effect, the name of the new corporation, the number and names of the directors and other officers thereof, and who shall be the first directors and officers, and their places of residence, the number of shares of the capital stock, the amount or par value of each share, and the manner of converting the capital stock of each of the said companies into that of the new corporation, and how and when directors and officers shall be chosen, with such other details as they shall deem necessary to perfect such new organization and the consolidation of said companies or railroads.

Second, said agreement shall be submitted to the stockholders of each of said companies or corporations at a meeting thereof called separately for the purpose of taking the same into consideration, due notice of the time and place of holding said meeting, and the object thereof shall be given by each company to its stockholders by written or printed notice addressed to each of the persons in whose names the capital stock of such company stands on the books thereof, and delivered to such persons respectively, or sent to them by mail when their postoffice address is known to the company, at least twenty days before the time of holding such meeting, and also by a general notice published daily or weekly for at least two months in some newspaper printed in the city, town or county where such company has its principal office or place of business ; or if no newspaper is there published, then in a newspaper published nearest to such city, town or county ; and at the said meeting of stockholders the agreement of the said directors shall be considered, and a vote by ballot taken for the adoption or rejection of the same, each share entitling the holder thereof to one vote, and said ballots shall be cast in person or by proxy, and if two-thirds of all the votes of all the stockholders shall be for the adoption of said agreement, then that fact shall be certified thereon by the secretaries of the respective companies under the seal thereof, and the agreement so adopted, or a certified copy thereof, shall be filed in the office of the Secretary of the Territory, and shall from thence be deemed and taken to be the agreement and act of consolidation of the said companies ; and a copy of the said agreement and act of consolidation duly certified by the Secretary of the Territory under his official seal, shall be evidence in all courts and places of the existence of said new corporation, and that the foregoing provisions of this act have been fully observed and complied with.

SEC. 5. Upon the making and perfecting such agreement and act of consolidation as hereinbefore provided, and filing the same or a copy thereof in the office of the Secretary of the Territory as aforesaid, the said corporations, parties thereto, shall be deemed and taken to be one corporation by the name provided in said agreement and act, but such act of consolidation shall not release such new corporation from any of the restrictions, disabilities or duties of the several corporations so consolidated.

SEC 6. Upon the consummation of said act of consolidation as aforesaid, all and singular the rights, privileges, exemptions and franchises of each of said corporations, parties to the same, and all the property, real, personal and mixed, and all the debts due on whatever account to either of said corporations, as well as all stock, subscriptions, provided that subscribers to unpaid stock in either company prior to consolidation shall, at their option, take stock so subscribed or not, and other things on action belonging to either of said corporations, shall be taken and deemed to be transferred to and vested in such new corporation, without further act or deed; and all claims, demands, property, right of way and every other interest shall be as effectually the property of the new corporation as they were of the former corporations, parties to the said agreement and act, and the title to all real estate, taken by deed or otherwise, under the laws of this Territory, vested in either of such corporations, parties to said agreement and act, shall not be deemed to revert or be in any way impaired by reason of this act, or anything done by virtue thereof, but shall be vested in the new corporation by virtue of such act of consolidation.

SEC. 7. The rights of all creditors of, and all liens upon, the property of either of said corporations, parties to said agreement and act, shall be preserved unimpaired, and the respective corporations shall be deemed to continue in existence to preserve the same, and all debts and liabilities incurred by either of said corporations except mortgages shall thenceforth attach to such new corporation and be enforced against it and its property to the same extent as if said debts or liabilities had been incurred or contracted by it. No suit, action, or other proceeding now pending before any court or tribunal, in which either of said railroad companies is a party, shall be deemed to have abated or been discontinued by the agreement and act of consolidation as aforesaid, but the same may be conducted in the name of the existing corporations to final judgment, or such new corporation may be, by order of the court, on motion, substituted as a party. Suits may be brought and maintained against such new corporation in the courts of this Territory, for all causes of action, in the same manner as against other railroad corporations therein.

SEC. 8. That any corporation heretofore or hereafter formed under the laws of this Territory may at any time by resolution of their stockholders, at a regular or special meeting, change its corporate name. After said resolution shall have been adopted, the president of said company or corporation seeking to change its name, the secretary thereof shall sign a certificate, attested with the seal of said company, which shall state, substantially, that said company or corporation, by resolution duly adopted, agreed to change the original corporate name of said corporation to (whatever name agreed on), and under such new corporate name such corporation propose, from and after the date of said certificate, to do, carry on and transact all business pertaining to said corporation, which shall be filed in the office of the Secretary of the Territory, and immediately upon the filing of said certificate in the office of the secretary aforesaid, the name of the corporation shall be changed to the name set forth in said certificate.

SEC. 9. This act to take effect from and after its passage.

Approved January 30, 1872.

CHAPTER XIV.

AN ACT providing for the appointment of Appraisers to assess the value of Real Estate over which lines of Railways may pass.

Be it enacted by the Legislative Assembly of the Territory of New Mexico:

In case any company heretofore or hereafter formed and organized under the laws of this Territory shall be unable to agree for the purchase of any real estate required for the purposes and objects of its corporation, it shall have the right to acquire title to the same in the manner and by the proceedings prescribed in this act.

SECTION 1. For the purpose of acquiring such title, the said company may present a petition praying for the appointment of Commissioners of Appraisal, to the District Court, at any general or special term thereof held in the district in which the real estate described in the petition is situated, or to the Judge of said District Court in vacation. Such petition shall be signed and verified according to the rules and practice of such court. It must contain a description of the real estate which the company seeks to acquire ; and it must, in effect, state that the company is duly incorporated, and that it is the intention of the company in good faith, to construct and finish a railroad from and to the places named for that purpose in its articles of association ; that the company has surveyed the line or route of its proposed road, and made a map or survey thereof, by which such route or line is designated, and that they have located their said road according to such survey ; that the land described in the petition is required for the purpose of constructing or operating on the proposed road ; and that the company has not been able to acquire title thereto, and the reason of such inability. The petition must also state the names and places of residence of the parties, so far as the same can by reasonable diligence be ascertained, who own or have, or claim to own or have estates or interest in the said real estate ; and if any such persons are infants, their ages, as near as may be, must be stated ; and if any of such persons are idiots, or persons of unsound mind, or are unknown, the fact must be stated, together with such other allegations and statements of liens or incumbrances on said real estate as the company may see fit to make. A copy of such petition, with a notice of the time and place the same will be presented to the District Court or Judge aforesaid, must be served on all persons whose interests are to be affected by the proceedings, at least ten days prior to the presentation of the same to the said court.

1st. If the person on whom such service is to be made, resides in this Territory, and is not an infant, idiot or person of unsound mind, service of a copy of such petition and notice must be made on him or his agent or attorney, authorized to contract for the sale of the real estate described in the petition, personally or by leaving the same at the usual place of residence of the person on whom service must be made aforesaid with some person of suitable age.

2d. If the person on whom such service is to be made resides out of the Territory, and has an agent residing in the Territory, authorized to contract for the sale of the real estate described in the petition, such service may be made on such agent, or on such person personally out of the Territory ; or it may be made by publishing conspicuously the notice, stating briefly the object of the application, and giving a description of the land to be taken in the paper of the largest circulation printed in the county in which the land to be taken is situated, and if no paper is printed in the county in which such land is situated, then the paper published nearest to such county, once in each week, for three months next previous to the presentation of the petition, and if the residence of such person residing out of this Territory, is known, or can, by reasonable diligence be ascertained, the company must, in addition to such publication as aforesaid, deposit a copy of the petition and notice in the postoffice, properly folded and directed to such person at the postoffice nearest his place of residence, at least ninety days before presenting such petition to the court, and pay the postage, chargeable thereon, to the United States.

3d. If any person on whom such service is to be made is under the age of twenty-one years, and resides in the Territory, such service shall be made as aforesaid on his general guardian ; and if he has no such guardian, then on such infant personally, if he is over the age of fourteen years ; and if under that age, then on the person who has the care of, or with whom such infant resides.

4th. If any person on whom such service to be made is an idiot, or of unsound mind, and resides in this Territory, such service may be made on the committee of his person or estate : or if he has no such committee, then on the person who has the care and charge of such idiot or person of unsound mind.

5th. If t he person on whom such service is to be made is unknown or his residence is unknown and cannot by reasonable diligence be ascertained, then such service may be made under the direction of the court, by publishing a notice stating the time and place the petition will be presented, the object thereof, with a description of the land to be affected by the proceedings, in a paper printed in the county where the land is situated, and if no paper is printed in the county in which such land is situated, then in the paper of the largest circulation published nearest to such county, once in each week for three months previous to the presentation of such petition.

6th. In case any party to be affected by the proceedings is an infant, idiot or of unsound mind, and has no general guardian or committee, the Court shall appoint a special guardian or committee to attend to the interest of such person in the proceedings, but if a general guardian or committee has been appointed for such person in the Territory, it shall be the duty of such general guardian or committee to attend to the interests of such infant, idiot or person of unsound mind ; and the Court shall require such security to be given by such general or special guardian or committee, as it may deem necessary to protect the rights of such infant, idiot or person of unsound mind ; and all notices required to be served in the progress of the proceedings, may be served on such general or special guardian or committee.

7th. In all cases not herein otherwise provided for, services of ·orders, notices, and other papers in the proceedings by this act, may be made as the District Court or Judge thereof shall direct.

SEC. 2. On presenting such petition to the District Court or Judge thereof, as aforesaid, with proof of service of a copy thereof and notice as aforesaid, all or any of the persons whose estates and interests are to be affected by the proceedings, may show cause against granting the prayer of the petition, and may disprove any of the facts alleged in it. The Court or Judge thereof shall hear the proofs and allegations of the parties, and if no sufficient cause is shown against granting the prayer of the petition, it shall make an order for the appointment of three disinterested and competent freeholders, each one of whom shall have resided in the county for at least three years, where the premises to be appraised are situated, three commissioners to ascertain and appraise the compensation to be made to the owners or persons interested in the real estate proposed to be taken in such county for the purposes of the company, and to fix the time and place for the first meeting of the commissioners.

SEC. 3. The commissioners shall take and subscribe an oath (Section 16) to faithfully discharge the duties required of them in the foregoing section — any one of them may issue subpœnas and administer oaths to witnesses; a majority of them may adjourn the proceedings before them from time to time, in their discretion. Whenever they meet, except by the appointment of the Court or pursuant to adjournment, they shall cause reasonable notice of such meetings to be given to the parties interested, or their agent or attorney. They shall view the premises described in the petition, and hear the proofs and allegations of the parties, and reduce the testimony taken by them, if any, to writing, and after the testimony in each case is closed, they, or a majority of them, all being present, shall, without any unnecessary delay, and before proceeding to the examination of any other claim, ascertain and determine the compensation which ought justly to be made by the company to the owners or persons interested in the real estate appraised by them ; and in fixing the amount of such compensation, said commissioners shall not make any allowance or deduction on account of any real or supposed benefits which the parties interested may derive trom the construction of the proposed railroad, or the construction of the proposed improvement connected with such road, for which such real estate may be taken. They, or a majority of them, shall also determine what sum ought to be paid to the general or special guardian or committee of an infant, idiot or person of unsound mind, or to any attorney appointed by the Court to attend to the interests of any unknown owner or party in interest, not personally served with notice of the proceedings, and who has not appeared for costs, expenses and counsel fees. The said commissioners shall make a report of their proceedings to the District Court at any general or special term, with the minutes of the testimony taken by them, if any; and they shall each be entitled to five dollars for services and expenses for every day they are actually engaged in the performance of their duties; to be paid by the company; except where the owners or persons interested in the real estate fail to have awarded them more than the amount of compensation offered them by the company before the appointment of commissioners, then to be paid by the said owners or persons interested, or if not paid by them to be paid by the company and deducted from the amount awarded.

SEC. 4. On such report being made by said commissioners the company shall give notice to the parties or their attorneys to be affected by the proceedings, according to the rules and practice of said Court at the next general or special term thereof, for the confirmation of such report; and the Court shall thereupon confirm such report, and shall make an order, containing a recital of the substance of the proceedings in the matter of the appraisal, and a description of the real estate appraised for which compensation is to be made; and shall also direct to whom money is to be paid or in what place and in what manner it shall be deposited by the company.

SEC. 5. A certified copy of the order so to be made as aforesaid, shall be recorded at full length in the office of the Probate Clerk of the county in which the land described in it is situated; and thereupon, and on the payment or deposit by the company of the sums to be paid as compensation for the land, and for costs, expenses and counsel fees as aforesaid, and as directed by said order, the company shall be entitled to enter upon, take possession of, and use the land for the purposes of the corporation, during the continuance of its corporate existence, by virtue of this or any other act; and all persons who have been made parties to the proceedings shall be divested and barred of all right, estate and interest in such real estate, during the corporate existence of the company as aforesaid. All real estate required by the company under and pursusnt to the provisions of this act, for the purposes of its incorporation, shall be deemed to be acquired for the public use. Within twenty days after the confirmation of the report of the commissioners, such appeal shall be heard by the District Court at the next special or general term thereof on such notice thereof being given according to the rules and practices of said court. On the hearing of such appeal, the Court may direct a new appraisal before new commissioners in its discretion ; the second report shall be final and conclusive on all the parties interested. If the amount of the compensation to be made by the company is increased by the second report, the difference shall be a lien on the land appraised and shall be paid by the company to the parties entitled to the same, or shall be deposited in such place as the Court shall direct ; and if the amount is diminished, the difference shall be refunded to the company by the party to whom the same may have been paid ; and judgment therefor, may be rendered by the Court on the filing of a second report against the party liable to pay the same. Such appeal shall not affect the possession by such company of the land appraised, and when the same is made by others than the company, it shall not be heard, except on a stipulation of the party appealing not to disturb such possession.

SEC. 6. If there are adverse and conflicting claimants to the money, or any part of it, to be paid as compensation for the real estate taken, the Court may direct the money to be paid into the said Court by the company, and may determine who is entitled to the same, and direct to whom the same shall be paid ; and may, in its discretion, order a reference to ascertain the facts on which such determination and order are to be made.

SEC. 7. The Court shall appoint some competent attorney to appear for and protect the rights of any party in interest who is unknown, and who has not appeared in the proceedings by attorney or agent. The Court shall also have power at any time to amend any defect or informality in any of the proceedings authorized by this act, as may be necessary ; or to cause new parties to be added, and to direct such further notices to be given to any party interested, as it deems proper ; and the Court, or the Judge thereof, shall have power to appoint other commissioners in place of any who shall die, or refuse or neglect to serve, or be incapable of serving.

SEC. 8. If at any time after an attempt to acquire title by the appraisal of damages or otherwise, it shall be found that the title thereby attempted to be acquired is defective, the company may proceed anew to acquire or perfect such title, in the same manner as if no appraisal had been made ; and at any stage of such new proceeding, the Court may authorize the corporation, if in possession, to continue in possession, and if not in possession, to take possession, and use such real estate during the pendency and until the final conclusion of such new proceedings ; and may stay all actions or proceedings against the com.

pany on account thereof, on such company paying into Court a sufficient sum, or giving security as the Court may direct, to pay the compensation therefor when finally ascertained; and in every such case, the party interested in such real estate may conduct the proceedings to a conclusion, if the company delays or omits to prosecute the same.

SEC 9. This act to take effect from and after its passage and approval.

Approved January 30, 1872.

CHAPTER XXX.

AN ACT authorizing counties to aid in the construction of Railroads.

Be it enacted by the Legislative Assembly of the Territory of New Mexico:

SECTION 1. That it shall be lawful for the people of any county in this Territory to pledge the credit of such county to borrow money, to issue bonds or other evidences of debt, to assist in the construction of any railroad passing through all or a portion of said county, for such amount or amounts of money not exceeding for any such road five per centum of the assessed value of the real and personal property of such county as the electors of said county may determine in meetings or elections that may be held in the various precincts of such county for that purpose, and at said meetings or elections the terms and conditions of such pledge of credit may also be determined as hereinafter provided in this act. The amount of bonds or other evidences [of debt] that may become due in any year shall not exceed two per centum of the assessed value of the property of such county at the time of issuing such bonds or other evidences of debt. Nor shall the rate of interest upon such bonds or other evidence of debt be more than .... per centum per annum.

SEC. 2. It shall be the duty of the probate judge or commissioner who may be hereafter provided by law, as the case may be, to call a meeting or election of the electors of the various precincts of said county who own taxable property, upon the written or printed, or in part written or printed request of fifteen owners of property electors and tax payers of such county, which request shall specify the amount which has to be raised or pledged, and the manner of raising and pledging the same by bonds or otherwise the rate of interest which has to be paid, the time or times of the payment and such other matters as they may consider for the welfare and security of the people of the county, and in publishing notices of the meetings or elections to be held in such county there shall also be published with such notice a copy of the request and names upon the same for which they call the meetings or elections. The questions submitted to the electors shall be those contained in the call for the meetings or elections, and those who vote upon the question of aid shall vote a ticket upon which is written or printed, or part written and part printed, the words—"Aid for railroads, yes," and those who vote in the negative shall vote a ticket on which is written or printed, or part written or printed, the words—"Aid for railroads, no." The elections or meetings to determine the question of aid shall be held at the usual places of voting in the precincts of the county to be called in the same manner, at the same hours of the day the polls shall be opened and shall be closed at the same time and manner, and the tickets shall be counted by the same inspectors and persons and they shall make returns of the same, certified, delivered or returned in the same manner to all intents and purposes as correct as is possible as in the case of annual elections heretofore held for the election of officers, except that four notices of elections printed in both languages Spanish and English shall be published at least fifteen days before the day of the election in some conspicuous place in every and each precinct in the county, and shall be published in some periodical published in the county.

SEC. 3. Should it be determined in such meetings or elections to aid in the construction of any railroad, and should it so appear from the proper returns of such meetings or elections held in such precincts as aforesaid, which returns shall be made, certified and delivered by the proper inspectors, to the same person or persons and in the same manner that ordinary returns of election of county officers are certified, made and delivered, within ten days afterwards, that such meetings or elections are held, it shall be the duty of the probate judge of such county or of any commissioner or commissioners who may by law be provided for, elected or appointed for that purpose to execute bonds or other evidences of debt, under their seal of office attested by the clerk of the Probate Court in conformity with the vote given at such elections or meetings of said county, and to require of the railroad company for whose benefit the aid has been voted such stock or other security for the same as can by such vote be required as a condition precedent for the delivery of such bonds or other evidences of debt and to do all other acts necessary to comply with the vote of the electors of such county, and all moneys, certificates, securities or other things inuring to said county under this act, and by virtue of the conditions of such vote of said electors shall be deposited with said probate judge or commissioners as the case may be, and by him or them shall be kept in safety until delivered in conformity with the law to the proper person at any time entitled thereto or to the successor in office of said probate judge or commissioners as aforesaid.

SEC. 4. It shall be the duty of the proper officer levying the usual taxes for territorial and county purposes under the general law of taxation, to raise by taxation such sums of money annually and from year to year as may be sufficient from time to time, to pay the principal and interest of such bonds or evidences of debt as regularly as the same shall become due, and in time to meet promptly the debt and interest : provided that no bonds or other evidences of debt created under this act shall be sold for less than their par value, nor such bonds or other evidences of debt shall be paid or delivered to any railroad company, nor to any person or persons for the use of such company, nor shall they be permitted to leave the hands of said judge or commissioners. except upon the certificate of the governor that the railroad to which such aid has been conceded has been completed in the county where such aid was voted, whether it shall be entirely for such part of the county as the road has to pass, or in such proportion to all the distance agreeably as the amount of bonds or other evidences of debt delivered shall show to the whole sum voted.

SEC. 5. This act shall take effect from and after its passage.

Approved February 1, 1872.

[Translation.]

CHAPTER XXXVII.

AN ACT to amend an act entitled an act, to create a general incorporation act, permitting persons to associate themselves together as bodies corporate for mining, manufacturing and other industrial pursuits.

CONTENTS.

Sec. 1. Objects additional, for which incorporate associations are permitted.

Be it enacted by the Legislative Assembly of the Territory of New Mexico:

SECTION 1. That the first section of an act approved December twenty-seventh, eighteen hundred and sixty-seven, entitled "An act to create a general incorporation act permitting persons to associate themselves together as bodies corporate, for mining, manufacturing and other industrial pursuits," shall be and hereby is amended to read as follows: corporations for mining, manufacturing or other industrial pursuits, or the construction or operation of railroads, wagon roads, irrigating ditches, and the colonization and improvement of lands in connection therewith, or for colleges, seminaries, churches, libraries, or any benevolent, charitable or scientific associations; may be formed according to the provisions of this act. Such corporation and the members thereof, being subject to all the conditions and liabilities herein imposed and to none others.

SEC. 2. This act shall take effect and be in force from and after its passage.

Approved January 5, 1876.

CHAPTER I.

AN ACT to provide for the incorporation of Railroad Companies, and the management of the affairs thereof, and other matters relating thereto.

TITLES.

[TITLE.]   Chapter I.

FORMATION OF RAILROAD CORPORATIONS.

Section 1. Articles of incorporation, who may enter into.
"   2. What must be set forth.
"   3. How executed.
"   4. Corporators must be subscribers to Capital Stock, and have
            paid in ten per cent.
"   5. Treasurer affidavit of subscriptions and per cent paid in
            must be attached to articles.
"   6. Articles of incorporation must be filed with Secretary of
            the Territory.
"   7. Owners of Capital Stock shall be called Stockholders.
"   8. Copy certified by the Secretary of the Territory received in
            evidence.

*Be it enacted by the Legislative Assembly of the Territory of New
Mexico*:

SECTION 1.   Railroad corporations may be formed by the voluntary
association of any five or more persons, in the manner prescribed in
this chapter.   Such persons must be citizens of the United States.

SEC. 2.   Articles of incorporation must be prepared, setting forth:

1st. The name of the corporation.

2d. The purpose for which it is formed.

3d. The place where its principal business is to be transacted.

4th. The term for which it is to exist, not exceeding fifty years.

5th. The number of its directors, which shall not be less than five
nor more than eleven; and the names and residences of the persons
who are appointed to act as such until their successors are elected and
qualified.

6th. The amount of its capital stock which (shall not exceed the amount actually required for the purposes of the corporation as estimated by competent engineers) and the number of shares into which it is divided.

7th. The amount of capital stock actually subscribed, and by whom.

8th. The termini of its road and intermediate branches.

9th. The estimated length of its road and of each of its branches.

10th. That at least ten per cent. of its capital stock subscribed has been paid to the treasurer of the intended corporation, giving his name and residence.

SEC. 3. The articles of incorporation must be subscribed by five or more persons, who must be citizens of the United States, and acknowledged by each of them before some officer authorized by the laws of this Territory to take and certify acknowledgments of conveyances of real property situated within this Territory. Each subscriber may subscribe said articles personally or by an attorney in fact, thereunto duly authorized in writing signed by said subscriber and acknowledged before some officer authorized by the laws of this Territory to take and certify acknowledgments of conveyances of real property situated within this Territory. All such powers of attorney must be securely attached to said articles of incorporation, and be filed therewith, as hereinafter provided.

SEC. 4. The corporators of each intended corporation before filing articles of incorporation must have actually subscribed to the capital stock of the corporation at least one thousand dollars for each mile of its road and branches, and at least ten per cent. thereof must have been paid for the benefit of the corporation, to a treasurer appointed by the subscribers to its articles of incorporation, or their attorneys in fact as aforesaid.

SEC. 5. There must be securely attached to said articles of incorporation an affidavit of the treasurer named therein, that the requisite amount of the capital stock of the intended corporation has been actually subscribed, and that ten per cent. thereof has been actually paid to him for the benefit of said corporation, stating the amount of stock subscribed, and the amount actually paid in.

SEC. 6. Said articles of incorporation, with the powers of attorney mentioned in the third section of this chapter, if any such there be, and the affidavit mentioned in the fifth section of this chapter, must be filed in the office of the Secretary of this Territory, and thereupon, the persons who have signed said articles, and their associates and successors, shall be a body politic and corporate, by the name stated in said articles for the term of years therein specified.

SEC. 7. The owners of shares of the capital stock of corporations formed under this act shall be called stockholders.

SEC. 8. A copy of any articles of incorporation filed in pursuance of the provisions of this chapter, certified by the Secretary of this Territory, must be received in all courts and other places as *prima facie* e .idence of the facts therein stated.

[TITLE.]   Chapter. II.

BY-LAWS.

Section 1. How adopted.
"   2. What to provide for.
"   3. Certified, Amendment and Repeal.   Recorded.

SECTION 1. Every corporation formed under this act must, within three months after filing articles of incorporation, adopt a code of by-laws for its government, not inconsistent with the laws of this Territory. By-laws may be adopted by stockholders representing a majority of all the subscribed capital stock, at a meeting of stockholders called for that purpose by order of the acting president, served upon them personally in writing, or by advertisement in some newspaper published in the county in which the principal place of business of the corporation is located, if there be one published therein, but if not, then in some paper published in some adjoining county. The time specified in said order for such meeting shall not be less than two weeks from the date thereof: *Provided*, that the written assent of the holders of two-thirds of the subscribed capital stock shall be effectual to adopt a code of by-laws without a meeting of the stockholders for that purpose.

SEC. 2. Where no other provision is especially made by this act, a corporation formed under it, may, by its by-laws provide for:

1st. The time, place and manner of calling and conducting the meetings of its directors and stockholders.

2d. The number of stockholders constituting a quorum at meetings of stockholders.

3d. The mode of voting by proxy at meetings of stockholders.

4th. The time for holding annual elections for directors and the mode and manner of giving notice thereof.

5th. The compensation and duties of officers.

6th. The manner of election and the tenure of office of all officers other than the directors.

7th. Suitable fines for violation of by-laws, not exceeding in any case one hundred dollars for any one offence; and—

8th. The mode and manner of collecting assessments, except as otherwise provided in this act.

Sec. 3. All by-laws must be certified by a majority of the directors and the secretary of the corporation, and copied in a legible hand in a book to be kept in the office of the secretary of the corporation to be known as the "Book of By-Laws," which shall be open to public inspection during office hours of each day except holidays. When recorded as aforesaid, the by-laws shall take effect, unless otherwise therein provided. By-laws may be amended or repealed, or new by-laws may be adopted at an annual meeting, or any other meeting of the stockholders called by the directors for that purpose, by a vote representing two-thirds of the subscribed capital stock, or the power to amend or repeal or adopt new by-laws, may, by a similar vote, at any such meeting, be delegated to the Board of Directors. Such power, when delegated, may be revoked by a similar vote at any regular meeting of the stockholders. Whenever any amendment or new by-law is adopted, it shall be copied in the "Book of By-Laws" immediately after the previous by-laws and shall not take effect until so recorded. If any by-law be repealed, the fact and date of repeal shall be noted in the "Book of By-Laws," and until so noted, the repeal shall not take effect.

[TITLE.]   Chapter III.

DIRECTORS, ELECTIONS AND MEETINGS.

Section 1. Members and Election of Directors.
"   2. Term of office, when elected.

Section 3. Conduct and what constitutes an election.
"   4. Business meetings, Quorums.
"   5. Dividends and Liabilities of Directors.
"   6. Removal of Directors from office.
"   7. When a justice of the peace may call a meeting of the stockholders.
"   8. Stockholders meetings must represent a majority of stock subscribed. Adjournments.
"   9. Stock belonging to insane persons or minors, how represented.
"   10. Provisions when failing to elect.
"   11. Recourse of persons aggrieved by an election.
"   12. Liability for false reports, certificates, etc.
"   13. Stockholders signing written consent to a meeting, makes it valid.
"   14. The same may elect officers to vacancies and transact business.
"   15. Must meet at principal place of business.
"   16. Calling of meetings, general and special.
"   17. Change of principal place of meeting.
"   18. Record of corporate debts. Book of Stockholders. Transfer books.

SECTION 1. The corporate powers, business and property of all corporations formed under this act must be exercised, conducted, controlled and managed by a board of not less than five nor more than eleven directors, to be elected from among the stockholders who are citizens of the United States. Unless a quorum be present and acting, no business performed or act done shall be valid or binding as against the corporation. Vacancies in the board of directors shall be filled by appointment by the board, unless otherwise provided by the by-laws of the corporation. Within the limits above specified, the number of directors may be increased or diminished by a vote of stockholders representing two-thirds of the subscribed capital stock, at any annual meeting of the stockholders.

SEC. 2. The directors named in the articles of incorporation shall hold their offices for one year from and after the date of the filing of said articles in the office of the Secretary of this Territory, as hereinbefore provided, or until their successors are elected and qualified. Thereafter, directors must be elected annually by the stockholders at such time as may be provided in the by-laws of the corporation. *Pro-*

vided, that if no time be fixed in the by-laws, such elections shall be had on the first Wednesday in July of each year.

Sec. 3. All elections of directors must be by ballot, and a vote of stockholders representing a majority of the subscribed capital stock shall be necessary to a choice. At all such elections, and at all other elections, and at all meetings of stockholders, each stockholder shall be entitled to one vote for each share of the capital stock owned by him.

Sec. 4. The directors named in the articles of incorporation must meet within one week after the filing of said articles at the principal place of business of the corporation, and organize by the election of a president who shall be one of their number, a secretary and treasurer; and their successors must so meet and organize immediately after their election. Directors must perform the duties enjoined upon them by law and the by-laws of the corporation. A majority of the directors shall constitute a board for the transaction of business, and every decision of a majority of the directors forming such board. made when duly assembled and in session as such board, shall be valid as a corporate act.

Sec. 5. The directors must not make or declare dividends, except from the surplus profits arising from the business of the corporation; nor must they withdraw, divide or pay to the stockholders, or any of them, any part of the capital stock; nor must they create debts beyond their subscribed capital stock, or reduce or increase the capital stock, except as hereinafter specially provided. For a violation of the provisions of this section, the directors under whose administration the same may have happened (except those who may have caused their dissent therefrom to be entered at large on the minutes of the proceedings of the directors at the time, or were not present when the same did happen) shall be, in their individual and private capacity, jointly and severally liable to the corporation, and to the creditors thereof, in the event of its dissolution, to the full amount of the capital stock so divided, withdrawn, paid out or reduced, or debt contracted; and no statute of limitations shall be a bar to any suit against such directors for any sums for which they are made liable by this section. There may, however, be a division and distribution of the capital stock and property of the corporation which may remain after the payment of all its debts, upon the dissolution of the corporation or the expiration of its term of existence.

Sec. 6. Directors may be removed from office by a vote of stockholders holding two-thirds of the subscribed capital stock, at a general meeting held after previous notice of the time and place and of the intention to propose such removal. Meetings of stockholders for this purpose may be called by the president or by a majority of the directors, or by stockholders holding at least one-half of the subscribed capital stock. Such calls must be in writing and addressed to the secretary who must thereupon give notice of the time, place and object of the meeting, and by whose order it is called. If the secretary refuse to give such notice, or if there be no secretary, the call may be addressed directly to the stockholders, and be served as a notice, in which case it must specify the time and place of meeting. The notice must be given in the manner prescribed in the by-laws. If, however, no provision has been made in the by-laws, then it shall be served in the manner prescribed in section 1, chapter 2 of this act. In case of removal, the vacancy may be immediately filled by election at the same meeting.

SEC. 7. Whenever, from any cause, there is no person authorized to call or preside at a meeting of the stockholders, any justice of the peace of the county where the principal place of business of the corporation is established, may, on written application of three or more of the stockholders, issue a warrant to one of the stockholders directing him to call a meeting of the stockholders, by giving the notice required in other cases; and said justice may in the same warrant direct such stockholder to preside at such meeting until a clerk is chosen and qualified, if there is no other officer present legally authorized to preside thereat.

SEC. 8. At all meetings of the stockholders for any purpose, a majority of the subscribed capital stock must be represented by the holders thereof, in person or by proxy, in writing. Every person acting thereat, in person, or by proxy, or by representative, must be a *bona fide* stockholder, having stock in his own name on the stock books of the corporation, at least ten days prior to the meeting. Any election or vote had other than in accordance with the provisions of this chapter shall be voidable at the instance of absent stockholders, and may be set aside upon petition to the District Court for the county where the same was had. Any regular or called meeting of the stockholders may be adjourned from day to day, or from time to time, if for any cause there are not present stockholders representing a majority of the subscribed stock, or no election or majority vote had. Such adjournments, and the reasons therefor shall be noted in the minutes of the proceedings of the meeting, which shall be recorded in the journal of proceedings of the board of directors.

SEC. 9. Shares of stock belonging to the estate of a minor or insane person, may be represented at all meetings of the stockholders by his guardian ; and of a deceased person, by his executor or administrator.

SEC. 10. If from any cause an election does not take place on the day appointed in the by-laws, or if no day be appointed in the by-laws, then on the day appointed in section two of this chapter, it may be held on any day thereafter as is provided for in such by laws, or to which such election may be adjourned or ordered by the directors. If an election has not been held at the appointed time, and no adjourned or other meeting for the purpose has been ordered by the directors a meeting may be called by the stockholders, as provided in section six of this chapter.

SEC. 11. Upon the application of any person or body corporate aggrieved by any election held by any corporation formed under this act, or any proceedings thereof, the District Judge of the district in which such election has been held must proceed forthwith summarily to hear the allegations and proofs of the parties, or otherwise, inquire into the matters complained of; and thereupon confirm the election, order a new one, or direct such other relief in the premises as accords with right and justice. Before any proceedings are had under this section, five days' notice thereof must be given to the adverse party, or those to be affected thereby.

SEC. 12. Any officer of a corporation formed under this act who wilfully gives a certificate, or wilfully makes an official report, or gives public notice, or makes an entry in any of the records or books of the corporation concerning the corporation or its business, which is false in any material representation, shall be liable for all the damages resulting therefrom to any person injured thereby ; and if two or more officers unite or participate in the commission of any of the acts herein designated, they shall be jointly and severally liable for such damages.

SEC. 13. When all the stockholders are present at any meeting, however called or notified, and sign a written consent thereto on the record of such meeting, the doings of such meeting shall be as valid as if had at a meeting otherwise legally called and noticed.

SEC. 14. The stockholders, when assembled, as provided in the last section, may elect officers to fill all vacancies then existing, and may act upon such other business as may lawfully be transacted at regular meetings of the stockholders.

SEC. 15. The meetings of stockholders and board of directors must be held at the office or principal place of business of the corporation.

SEC. 16. When no provision is made in the by-laws for regular meetings of the directors and the mode of calling special meetings, all meetings of the directors must be called by special notice in writing, to be given to each director by the secretary, on the order of the president, or if there be no president, on the order of any two directors. Such orders and notice shall be recorded in the journal of the proceedings of the board of directors.

SEC. 17. Every corporation formed under this act, may change its principal place of business from one place to another in the same county, or from one city or county to another city or county within this Territory. Before such change is made, the assent, in writing, of the holders of two-thirds of the subscribed capital stock must be obtained and filed in the office of the secretary of the corporation. When such consent is obtained and filed, notice of the intended removal or change must be published at least once a week for three successive weeks, in some newspaper published in the county wherein said principal place of business is situated, if there is one published therein ; if not, in a newspaper published in an adjoining county, giving the name of the county or city, or town where it is situated, and that to which it is intended to remove it.

SEC. 18. The directors must cause a book to be kept by the secretary to be called " Record of Corporation Debts," in which the secretary shall record all written contracts of the directors, and a succinct statement of the debts of the corporation, the amount thereof and to whom contracted, which book shall at all times be open to inspection by any stockholder, or other party in interest. When any contract or debt shall be paid or discharged, the secretary shall make a memorandum thereof in the margin, or in some other convenient place in the record where the same is recorded. They must also cause a complete record to be kept by the secretary of the proceedings of all meetings of the board of directors and of the stockholders, in a book provided specially for that purpose. Such record must show the name of each director present at the opening of each meeting of the board, and at what stage of the proceedings any director not present at the opening appeared, and also at what stage of the proceedings any director may absent himself on leave or otherwise. The record must also show the name of each director voting against any proposition, whenever any director may require the same to be placed upon the record. Prior to the adjournment of each meeting of the board or of the stockholders, as the case may be, the record of the proceedings of such meeting must be read and approved. The directors must also cause such other books to be kept by the secretary as may be deemed necessary, or prescribed by the directors, in which all the business transactions of the corporation must be plainly and accurately entered and kept; also a book to be labeled "Book of Stockholders," which shall contain the names of all persons, alphabetically arranged, who are, or shall have been, stockholders of the corporation, showing their places of residence, if known, the number of shares of stock held by them respectively, the time when they, respectively, became the owners of such shares, the amount of cash actually paid to the company by them respectively for their stock; and also the time when they may have ceased to be stockholders. Said "Book of Stockholders," during the office hours of the secretary, shall be open to the inspection of stockholders and creditors of the corporation and their personal representatives. The directors must also cause to be kept by the secretary a book to be labeled "Transfer Book," in which all transfers of stock must be entered. Said "Transfer Book" shall be received in all courts and places as *prima facie* evidence of the facts therein stated.

[TITLE.] Chapter IV.

CORPORATE STOCK.

Section 1. Shares of stock, personal property, and how and when may be transferred.
" 2. Issues of certificates of stock.
" 3. Shares held by married women.
" 4. Shares of stock held by non-residents.

SECTION I. Shares of the capital stock of any corporation formed under this act shall be personal property, and may be transferred by endorsement, by the signature of the proprietor, or his attorney or legal representative and delivery of the certificate; but such transfer shall not be valid, except between the parties thereto, until the same shall have been entered upon the "Transfer Book" of the corporation so as to show the names of the parties by and to whom transferred, the number or designation of the shares and the date of transfer. *Provided* no stock shall be transferred upon the "Transfer Book" of the corporation until all previous assessments thereon shall have been fully paid in, nor shall any such transfer be valid except as between the parties thereto, unless at least twenty per cent. shall have been paid thereon, and certificates issued therefor, and the transfer approved by the Board of Directors, except by consent of the Board of Directors.

SEC. 2. Certificates for stock, when fully paid up, signed by the president and secretary, shall be issued to the owners thereof, and provision may be made in the by-laws for issuing certificates prior to full payment, under such restrictions, and for such purposes, as the by-laws may provide.

SEC. 3. Shares of stock held or owned by a married woman may be transferred by her, her agent, or attorney, without the signature of her husbaand, in the same manner as if such married woman were a *femme sole.* All dividends payable upon any shares of stock held by a married woman may be paid to such married woman, her agent or attorney, in the same manner as if she were unmarried, and it shall not be necessary for her husband to join in any receipt therefor, and any proxy or power given by a married woman touching any stock owned by her, shall be valid and binding without the signature of her husband, the same as if she were unmarried.

SEC. 4. When shares of stock are owned by persons residing out of the Territory, the president, secretaay or directors of the corporation, before entering any transfer thereof on the books, or issuing a certificaté therefor to the transferee, may require from the attorney or agent of the non-resident owner, or from the person claiming under the transfer, an affidavit or other evidence that the non-resident owner was alive at the date of the transfer, and that his signature to the transfer is genuine ; and if such affidavit or other satisfactory evidence be not furnished, may require from the attorney, agent or claimant, a bond of indemnity with two sureties, satisfactory to the board of directors : or if not so satisfactory, then one approved by a district or county judge, of the county in which the principal office of the corporation is situated, conditioned to protect and indemnify the corporation against any liability to the non-resident owner or his or her legal representatives, in case of his or her death before the transfer, and if such affidavit or other evidence, or bond, be not furnished when required as herein provided, neither the corporation, nor any officer thereof, shall be liable for refusing to enter the transfer on the books of the corporation.

[TITLE.] Chapter V.

ASSESSMENTS.

SECTION 1. The directors may call in and demand from the stock-holders the sums by them subscribed, in installments of not more than ten per cent per month: *Provided*, that if the whole capital stock has not been paid in, and the corporation is unable to meet its liabilities, or to satisfy the claims of its creditors, the assessment may be for the full amount unpaid; or if a less amount is sufficient, then it may be for such a per centage as will raise that amount. Notice of each assessment shall be given to the stockholders personally or shall be published once a week for at least four weeks in a newspaper published at the place designated as the principal place of business of the corporation, or if none be published there in some newspaper nearest to such place, which notice shall be substantially in the following form :

" Notice is hereby given that an assessment of —— dollars per share on the capital stock of —— corporation is due and payable at the office of the corporation in —— (and at such other places as the directors may designate, naming them,) within thirty days from date. All stockholders are requested to make payment on or before that time, or such assessments will be promptly collected in the manner prescribed by law, and the by-laws of said corporation.

(Signed) ...., Secretary."

If after such notice shall have been given, any stockholder shall make default in the payment of the assessment upon the shares held by him, the same may be collected by suit in any court of competent jurisdiction, in the name of the corporation ; or so many of such shares may be sold as may be necessary for the payment of the assessment on all the shares held by him. The sale of said shares shall be made as prescribed in the by-laws of the corporation : *Provided*, that no sale shall be made except at public auction, to the highest bidder ; and, at such sale, the person who will agree to pay the assessment so due, together with the expenses of advertisement and all other expenses of the sale for the smallest number of whole shares, shall be deemed to be the highest bidder. All stock shall be liable to such sale, and all stockholders, shall be liable to recovery by action at law, as aforesaid.

SEC. 2. No assessment shall be levied while any portion of a previous one remains unpaid, unless—

1st. The power of the corporation has been exercised in accordance with the provisions of this chapter, for the purpose of collecting such previous assessment.

2d. The collection of the previous assessment has been enjoined ; or—

3d. The assessment falls within the first proviso contained in section 1 of this chapter.

SEC. 3. All shares sold for assessments as provided in section 1 of this chapter, shall be transferred to the purchaser on the "Transfer Book" of the corporation on payment of the assessment and costs.

SEC. 4. If, at a sale, no bidder offers the amount of the assessments, costs and charges due, the stock may be bid in and purchased by the corporation, through the secretary, president or any director thereof, at the amount of the assessments. costs and charges due ; and the amount of the assessments, costs and charges shall be credited as paid in full on the books of the corporation and an entry of the transfer of the stock to the corporation must be made on the "Transfer Book" thereof. While the stock remains the property of the corporation, it shall not be assessable nor shall any dividends be declared thereon ; but all assessments and dividends shall be apportioned upon the stock held by the stockholders of the corporation.

SEC. 5. All purchases of its own stock made by any corporation as provided in the last section shall vest the legal title to the same in the corporation ; and the stock so purchased shall be held subject to the control of the stockholders, who may make such disposition of the same as they may deem proper, in accordance with the by-laws of the corporation, or by vote of the stockholders representing a majority of all the remaining shares. Whenever any portion of the capital stock of a corporation is held by the corporation by purchase as aforesaid, a majority of the remaining shares shall be a majority of the stock for all purposes of election, or voting on any question at the meeting of the stockholders.

SEC. 6. The dates fixed in any notice of assessment, or notice of delinquent sale may be extended from time to time for not more than thirty days, by order of the directors entered in the journal of their proceedings ; but no order extending the time for the performance of any act specified in any notice shall be effectual unless notice of such extension or postponement is appended to and published with the notice to which the order relates.

SEC. 7. No assessment shall be invalidated by a failure to make publication of the notice thereof hereinbefore provided for, or *by* any notice required by the by-laws of the corporation, nor by the non-performance of any act required in order to enforce the payment of the same ; but in case of any substantial error or omission in the course of proceedings for collection, all previous proceedings except the levying of the assessment shall be void and publication shall be begun anew.

SEC. 8. No action shall be sustained to recover stock sold for delinquent assessments, upon the ground of irregularity in the assessments, irregularity or defect in the notice of sale, or in the sale, unless the party seeking to maintain such action first pays or tenders to the corporation or the party holding the stock sold, as the case may be, the sum for which the same was sold, together with all subsequent assessments which may have been paid thereon, and interest on such sums from the time they were paid ; and no such action shall be sustained unless the same shall be commenced by the filing of a complaint and the issuing of a summons thereon within six months after such sale shall have been made.

SEC. 9. The publication of notices required by this chapter or by the by-laws of the corporation may be proved by the affidavit of the printer, foreman or principal clerk of the newspaper in which the same shall have been published ; and the affidavit of the secretary or auctioneer shall be *prima facie* evidence of the time and place of sale, of the quantity and particular description of the stock sold, and to whom and for what price, and of the fact of the purchase money being paid. The affidavits must be filed in the office of the corporation, and copies of the same, certified by the secretary under the corporate seal, shall be *prima facie* evidence of the facts therein stated in all courts and other places.

[TITLE.] Chapter VI.

CORPORATE POWERS.

Section 1. Defined.
"   2. Additional powers. 1st. Routes and Surveys. 2-3. To
take, hold and convey donations for use in business. 4th.
May occupy land and take material. 5th. May construct
railway along streams, highways, etc., etc. 6th. Cross,
intersect and join other railroads. 7th. Take private
property necessary. 8th. Transport persons and property, erect necessary buildings and other acccessaries. 9th.
Take and possess water. 10th. Regulate time and rates
of transportation. Limitation, extra hazardous goods.
11th. Speed, and rules governing employees. 12th. Violation of rules and expulsion from cars. 13th. Negotiate
loans and give bonds and mortgages. 14-15. To lease
and grant leases of railways. Telegraph lines. 16th.
To change line of road. 17th. To increase or diminish
capital stock. 18th. To consolidate with other lines, and
what articles of incorporation and consolidation, shall set
forth. 19th. Additional and general.
"   3. Property of infants, idiots or insane necessary, How acquired.

SECTION 1. Every corporation formed under this act as such shall
have power:
1. Of succession by its corporate name for the period limited in its
articles of incorporation.
2. To sue and be sued in any court.
3. To make and use a common seal, and alter the same at pleasure.
4. To acquire, purchase, hold and convey such real and personal
estate as the purposes of the corporation may require.
5. To appoint such subordinate officers or agents as the business
of the corporation may require, and to allow them suitable compensation.
6. To make by-laws not inconsistent with any existing law, for the
management of its business and property, the regulation of its affairs,
and for the transfer of its stock.
7. To admit stockholders and to sell their stock or shares for the payment of assessments or instalments.

8. To construct, maintain and operate telegraph lines in connection with its railroad branches.

9. To enter into any obligations or contracts necessary or convenient to the transaction of its ordinary affairs, or for carrying out the purposes of the corporation; and *generally*, such corporation shall have, and possess, for the purpose of constructing, maintaining and operating its railroads and telegraph lines, and carrying on its business, all the rights, powers and privileges which are enjoyed by natural persons.

SEC. 2. In addition to the foregoing, every corporation formed under this act shall have the following powers:

1. To cause such examinations and surveys to be made as may be necessary to the selection of the most suitable routes for its railroad and telegraph lines, and for that purpose, by its officers and agents, to enter upon the lands and waters of the Territory, of private persons, and of private and public corporations, subject, however, to responsibility for all damages which it may do thereto.

2. To take, hold and convey, by deed or otherwise, the same as a natural person, such voluntary grants and donations of real and personal property as may be made to aid the construction and maintenance, and to provide for the accommodation of its railroad and telegraph lines, or either thereof.

3. To purchase, and, by voluntary grants and donations, to receive and take, and by its officers, engineers, surveyors and agents, to enter upon, possess, hold and use in any manner it may deem proper, all such lands and other property as its directors may deem necessary, proper and convenient, for the construction, maintenance and operation of its railroad and telegraph lines, or either thereof, and for the erection of stations, depots, water tanks, side tracks, turnouts, turntables, yards, workshops, warehouses, and for all other purposes necessary or convenient to said corporation in the transaction of its business.

4. To lay out its railroad and branches, not exceeding two hundred feet wide, and to construct and maintain the same, with a single or double track, with such appendages as its directors may deem necessary for the convenient use thereof. For the purposes of making embankments, excavations, ditches, drains, culverts and the like, and of procuring timber, stone, gravel and other materials for the proper construction and security of its railroad and branches, such corporation may take and occupy as much more land as its directors may deem necessary or convenient for the purposes aforesaid.

5. To construct its railroads and telegraphs across, along or upon

any stream of water, water-course, street, avenue or highway, or across
any railway, canal, ditch or flume which its railway and telegraph, or
either thereof, shall intersect, cross or run along ; but such corporation
shall restore such stream, water-courses, streets, avenues, highways,
railways, canals, ditches and flumes, so intersected, to their former
state, as near as may be, so as not to unnecessarily impair their use or
injure their franchises : and wherever its road shall cross a navigable
stream or body of water, the bridge shall be constructed with a draw,
if a draw be necessary to avoid obstructing the navigation of such
stream or body of water.

6. To cross, intersect, join and unite its railroad with any other railroads that have been heretofore constructed, or that may be hereafter
constructed, at any point or points on the routes thereof, and upon
the grounds of such other railroad companies, with the necessary turnouts, sidings and switches and such other conveniences and appliances
as may be necessary to make and complete said crossings, intersections
and connections ; and such other railroad companies shall unite with
the directors of such corporation in making said crossings, intersections
and connections, and shall grant the facilities therefor upon such terms
and conditions as may be agreed upon between them ; but if they are
unable to agree upon the compensation to be made therefor, or the
points at which, or the manner in which such crossings, intersections
and connections shall be made, the same shall be ascertained, determined and declared in the manner and by the proceedings hereinafter
provided, for the taking of private property for the use of such corporation.

7. To purchase or take by donation or otherwise, lands, timber,
stone, gravel and other materials to be used in the construction and
maintenance of its railroads and telegraphs, or either thereof ; and if
the same cannot be obtained by agreement with the owners thereof, to
take the same by the proceedings and in the manner hereinafter provided for the taking of private property for the use of such corporation.

8. To take, transport, carry and convey persons and property on its
railroads, by the force and power of steam, of animals, or any other
mechanical power, or by any combination thereof, and to collect and
receive tolls as compensation therefor.

9. To erect and maintain all necessary and convenient buildings,
stations, depots, watering-places, fixtures and machinery for the accommodation of its passengers, freight and business, and to obtain and hold,

by purchase, donation or condemnation, as hereinafter provided, lands and other property necessary therefor.

10. To take, possess, and enjoy, by purchase, donation or condemnation, as hereinafter provided, such natural springs and streams of water, or so much thereof as may be necessary for its uses and purposes in operating its railroads, together with the right of way thereto for pipes, ditches, canals or aqueducts for the conveyance thereof.

11. To regulate the time and manner in which passengers and property shall be transported over its roads, and the tolls or compensation to be paid therefor: *Provided*, that it shall be unlawful for such corporation to charge more than ten cents per mile for each passenger, and fifteen cents per mile for each ton of 2,000 pounds, or forty cubic feet, of freight transported on its roads: *Provided further*, that in no case shall such corporation be required to receive less than twenty-five cents for any one lot of freight for any distance: *Provided further*, that such corporation shall not be required to transport domestic animals, nitro-glycerine compounds, gunpowder, acids, phosphorus and other explosive or destructive or combustible materials, except upon such terms, conditions and rates of freightage as its board of directors may from time to time prescribe and establish.

12. To regulate the force and speed of its locomotives, cars, trains or other machinery used on its roads, and to establish, execute and enforce all needful and proper rules and regulations for the management of its trains, the conduct of its business, and to secure the safety, comfort and good behavior of its passengers and employees and agents. And for the prevention and suppression of gambling of every kind and description on its cars, or within its depots or station grounds.

13. To expel from its cars at any stopping place, using no more force than may be necessary, any passenger who, upon demand, shall refuse to pay his fare; or shall behave in a rude, riotous or disorderly manner toward other passengers, or the employees of such corporation in charge of such cars, or, upon his attention being called thereto, shall persist in violating the rules of the corporation against gambling upon its cars.

14. To borrow, on the credit of the corporation, and under such regulations and restrictions as the directors thereof, by unanimous concurrence may impose, such sums of money as may be necessary for constructing and equipping its railroad and telegraph lines, and to issue and dispose of its bonds or promissory notes therefor in denominations of not less than five hundred dollars, an l at a rate of interest not exceeding ten per cent. per annum. And also to issue its bonds or

promissory notes of the same denomination and rate of interest in payment of any debts or contracts for constructing, equipping and completing its railroad and telegraph lines, and all else relating thereto. The amount of bonds or promissory notes issued for such purposes shall not exceed in all the amount of its capital stock ; and to secure the payment of such bonds or notes, it may mortgage its corporate property and franchises.

15. To lease the whole or any portion of its railroad and telegraph lines to any other corporation formed under this act, or to any corporation formed under the laws of any other state or territory, with the road of which, its road may connect and form a continuous line of travel and transportation ; or to grant to any such corporations the right to use in common with it, its railroad and telegraph lines, or any part thereof. In making such leases and grants, and in agreeing upon, and prescribing the terms and conditions thereof, and the amount and nature of the considerations therefor, such corporation shall have all the rights, powers, capacities, and abilities which are enjoyed by natural persons.

16. To take leases of such other railroad and telegraph lines as are mentioned in the last preceding subdivision of this section, and grants of right to use the same in common, and, in taking and receiving such leases and grants, to have and enjoy the same rights, powers, capacities and abilities which are granted in said last preceding subdivision of this section.

17. To change the line of its road, in whole or in part, whenever a majority of its directors may so determine, *provided*, no such change shall vary the general route of such road, as described in its articles of incorporation. The land required for such new line may be acquired by contract with the owners thereof, or by condemnation, as provided in this act, as in the case of the original line.

18. To increase or diminish its capital stock, if at any time it shall appear that the amount thereof as fixed in its articles of incorporation is either more or less than is actually required for constructing, equipping, operating and maintaining its road and telegraph lines. Such increase or decrease shall not be made except by a vote of stockholders representing at least two-thirds of the subscribed capital stock. A certified copy of the proceedings of the meeting, and its action in the premises, under the seal of the corporation, must be filed in the office of the Secretary of this Territory, and be by him attached to the articles of incorporation on file in his office.

19. To consolidate with one or more corporations formed under this act, or under the laws of any other state or territory, its capital stock,

properties, roads, equipments, adjuncts, franchises, claims, demands, contracts, agreements, obligations, debts, liabilities and assets of every kind and description upon such terms and in such manner as may be agreed upon by their respective boards of directors ; *provided*, no such consolidation shall take effect until the same shall have been ratified and confirmed in writing by stockholders of the respective corporations representing three fourths of the subscribed capital stock of their respective corporations. In case of such consolidation "Articles of Incorporation and Consolidation " must be prepared setting forth—

1st. The name of the new corporation.

2d. The purpose for which it is formed.

3d. The place where its principal business is to be transacted.

4th. ·The term for which it is to exist, which shall not exceed fifty years.

5th. The number of its directors (which shall not be less than five nor more than eleven) and the names and residences of the persons appointed to act as such until their successors are elected and qualified.

6th. The amount of its capital stock (which shall not exceed the amount actually required for the purposes of the new corporation, as estimated by competent engineers,) and the number of shares into which it is divided.

7th. The amount of stock actually subscribed, and by whom.

8th. The termini of its road or roads and branches.

9th. The estimated length of its road or roads and branches.

10th. That at least ten per cent. of its subscribed capital stock has been paid in.

11th. The names of the constituent corporations and the terms and conditions of consolidation in full. Said articles of incorporation and consolidation must be signed and countersigned by the presidents and secretaries of the several constituent corporations and sealed with their corporate seals. There must be annexed thereto memoranda of the ratification and confirmation thereof by the stockholders of each constituent corporation, which must be respectively signed by stockholders representing at least three-fourths of the capital stock of their respective corporations. When completed as aforesaid, said articles must be filed in the office of the Secretary of this Territory, and thereupon the constituent corporations named therein must be deemed and held to have become extinct in all courts and places, and said new corporation must be deemed and held in all courts and places to have succeeded to all their several capital stocks, properties, roads, equipments, adjuncts, franchises, claims, demands, contracts, agreements, assets, choses and rights in action of every kind and description, both at law and in equity, and to be entitled to possess, enjoy and enforce the same and every thereof, as fully and completely as either and every of its constituents might have done had no consolidation taken place. Said consolidated or new corporation must also, in all courts and places, be deemed and held to have become subrogated to its several constituents and each thereof, in respect to all their contracts and agreements with other parties, and all their debts, obligations and liabilities of every kind and nature, to any persons, corporations or bodies politic, whomsoever, or whatsoever, and said new corporation must sue and be sued in its own name in any and every case in which any or either of its constituents might have sued or might have been sued, at law or in equity, had no such consolidation been made. Such consolidated or new corporation shall possess, enjoy and exercise all its franchises, properties, powers, privileges, abilities, rights and immunities under the provisions of this act, and shall conduct its business according to its provisions, and be subject to all its pains and penalties. Nothing in this subdivision contained shall be construed to impair the obligations of any contract to which any of such constituents were parties at the date of such consolidation. All such contracts may be enforced by action or suit, as the case may be, against the consolidated corporation and satisfaction obtained out of the property which, at the date of the consolidation, belonged to the constituent which was a party to the contract in action or suit, as well as out of any other property belonging to the consolidated corporation.

20th. Every corporation formed under this act, in addition to the foregoing, shall have such further powers as may be necessary or convenient to enable it to exercise and enjoy, fully and completely, all the powers granted by this act; and, generally all such powers as are usually conferred upon, required and exercised by railroad corporations; and in the exercise of its powers and every thereof, shall have and enjoy all the rights, privileges, abilities and capacities which are enjoyed by natural persons.

SEC. 3. If it shall become necessary for any of the aforesaid purposes of such corporation, to acquire any land, or any right, title, interest or estate therein, which is the property of an infant, idiot or insane person, the guardian, executor or administrator, as the case may be, may sell and convey the same to such corporation; but such sale and conveyance shall not be valid, unless approved by the Probate Court, or the judge thereof, within whose jurisdiction such land shall be situated; and the judge of such court is hereby authorized to examine into the terms and conditions of such sales and conveyances, and if he finds them to be just, fair and proper, he shall enter his approval upon the records of said court, and indorse the same upon such conveyances, and, thereupon, such conveyances shall have the same force and effect as conveyances made by persons competent to convey in their own names. Should there be no guardian, executor or administrator competent to make such sale and conveyance, it shall be the duty of such judge, upon the petition of any relative or friend acting for the benefit and in the interest of such infant, idiot or insane person to appoint a guardian for the purpose of making such sale and conveyance, who shall be required to give a bond, with sureties to be approved by said judge, for the faithful performance of his trust. For the purpose of transacting the business provided for in this section, said court shall be deemed to be always open, and a complete record of its proceedings therein shall be kept as in other cases.

[TITLE.] Chapter VII.

EMINENT DOMAIN.

Section 1. Taking private property. Appraisal by commissioners. Award.

SECTION 1. In all cases where, by this act, any corporation formed under it is empowered to take for its use land, water, timber, stone, gravel or other materials, and the owner or claimant thereof and such corporation shall be unable to agree as to the compensation to be paid therefor, the amount shall be ascertained and determined by the appraisal of three disinterested commissioners, who shall be appointed upon the application of either party, and upon five days' notice to the other party, by the judge of the District Court in and for the district in which such land, water, timber, stone, gravel or other materials shall be situated; and said commissioners, in their assessment of compensation, shall appraise such premises or property at what would have been the value thereof, if the road for which the same shall be required had not been built; and upon return into court of such appraisement, and upon payment to the clerk thereof of the amount so awarded by the commissioners for the use and benefit of the owner thereof, the land, water, timber, stone, gravel or other materials so appraised shall be deemed to be taken by such corporation, which shall thereby acquire full title to the same for the uses and purposes aforesaid; and either party feeling aggrieved by said assessment may, within ten days after notice of the return thereof, file an appeal therefrom to said court, and demand a jury of twelve men to estimate the compensation to be paid; but such appeal shall not interfere with the right of such corporation to take possession of such property, and proceed with the construction of its road or other improvements. The party so appealing shall give bonds with sufficient surety or sureties, to be approved by said judge, for the payment of all costs which may arise upon such appeal. In case the party appealing does not obtain a more favorable verdict, such party shall pay the whole cost incurred by the other party as well as his own. The payment into court for the use of the owner or claimant, of a sum equal to that finally awarded shall be held to vest in such corporation title to the land, water or other property in question, and the right to occupy, take and use the same for any of the purposes aforesaid. In case any of the lands or other property to be taken, as aforesaid, shall be held by any person residing without the Territory, or subject to any legal disability, the court may appoint a proper person, who shall give bonds, with sufficient surety or sureties, to be approved by the judge, for the faithful execution of his trust, and such person may represent in court the person so absent or under legal disability, as aforesaid, when the same proceeding as aforesaid, shall be had in reference to the appraisement of the lands or other property in question, and with the same effect. The title of such corporation to the lands or other property taken by virtue of this act, shall not be affected or impaired by reason of the failure of the person so appointed to faithfully discharge his trust. In case it shall be necessary for such corporation to take lands or other property which are unoccupied, and of which there is no apparent owner or claimant, it may proceed to take and use the same for any of the purposes aforesaid, and may institute proceedings in the manner above described for the purpose of acquiring title thereto, and determining the compensation to be paid therefor; and said court shall prescribe and direct the kind of notice to be served on such owner or owners, and may, in its discretion, appoint an agent or guardian to represent such owner or owners, in case of his or their incapacity or non-appearance. Such owner or claimant shall be entitled to receive from such corporation the compensation so awarded upon demand made at any time within six years thereafter, and may have his action to recover the same ; but after the lapse of six years, all claim for such compensation shall be barred. Said court shall be always open for the transaction of the business provided for in this section, and shall transact the same with all reasonable dispatch.

[TITLE.] Chapter VIII.

REGULATION AND MANAGEMENT.

Section 18. May demand the payment ot fares and property in advance ; liability.
"   19. Map and profile of land acquired, etc., to be filed with the Secretary of the Territory.
"   20. Fences.
"   21. No fence required on public lands.
"   22. Annual report to be filed with Secretary of the Territory ; what it shall state.
"   23. Quality of rails. Gauge.
"   24. Construction to commence within two years.

SECTION 1. Every corporation formed under this act shall cause a bell of at least twenty pounds weight to be attached to each of its locomotives, and shall cause the same to be rung at a distance of not less than eighty rods from the crossing of any public street, road or highway, under a penalty of one hundred dollars, to be recovered by action in the name of the Territory, in any court of competent jurisdiction, one-half of which shall go to the informer and the other half of which shall go to the Territory ; and such corporation shall also be liable for all damages which may be sustained by any person by reason of a noncompliance with the provisions of this section.

SEC. 2. A check shall be affixed to every package or parcel of baggage when taken for transportation by such corporation, and a duplicate thereof shall be given to the passenger delivering the same for transportation, and, if such check be refused on demand, such corporation shall pay to such passenger the sum of twenty dollars, to be recovered by action in any court of competent jurisdiction ; and, in addition to the foregoing, no fare or toll shall be collected from such passenger ; and if such passenger shall have paid his or her fare, he or she shall be entitled, upon demand, to a return thereof. Upon the production of such check at his or her place of destination, such passenger shall be entitled to receive his or her said baggage, and if the same be not delivered within a reasonable time, he or she may be a witness in any action brought on account of such non-delivery, to prove the contents and value thereof ; *provided*, that all action to recover such baggage, or the value thereof, shall be barred at the expiration of three months after the same shall have accrued.

SEC. 3. Every corporation formed under this act shall safely and securely keep, as warehouseman, all unclaimed baggage for the space of three months, at the expiration of which time it may sell the same, if not previously called for, at public auction, after ten days' public notice by publication in some newspaper of general circulation; or if there be no such paper in the vicinity, then by posting written or printed notices in three conspicuous places in the neighborhood in which such sale is to be made. For the purpose of making such sale, it shall be lawful to open each trunk, package or parcel, and make known the contents thereof. A true account of the sale shall be kept, showing the price at which each parcel was sold, and the number thereof, which shall be the same as the number stamped upon the check thereto attached; and if there be any name, initial letters, or other marks upon such parcel, the same shall also be noted in said account. The proceeds of such sale shall be paid, less the expenses of the sale, to the owner, upon demand, and proof of ownership, at any time within sixty days after the sale, after which date all right of action therefor shall be barred.

SEC. 4. Every corporation formed under this act shall start and run its cars for the transportation of persons and property at such regular times as it shall fix by public notice, and shall furnish sufficient accommodations for all such persons and property as shall, within a reasonable time previous thereto, offer or be offered for transportation at the place of starting and the junction of other railroads and stopping-places established for taking and leaving persons and property, and shall transport between such places all such persons and property on the payment of its lawful charges therefor; provided, such corporation may decline to receive any person afflicted with any contagious disease, or otherwise unfit to be admitted into its cars.

SEC. 5. In case any corporation formed under this act shall refuse to transport persons or property as provided in section four of this chapter, or to leave the same at place of destination, it shall pay to the party aggrieved all damages he or she shall sustain thereby.

SEC. 6. It shall be unlawful for any corporation formed under this act, in making up its trains, to place mail, express, baggage or freight cars in the rear of passenger cars; and for every violation of this provision. the officer or agent by whom the same was done, or suffered to be done, shall be deemed guilty of a misdemeanor, and, upon conviction thereof, shall be fined in any sum not exceeding five hundred dollars, or imprisoned not exceeding three months, or both; and, should any accident happen to life or limb by reason of such unlawful arrangement of cars, he shall be deemed guilty of felony, and upon conviction thereof, shall be imprisoned in the penitentiary for any term not less than one nor more than five years.

SEC. 7. If a passenger be injured while on the platform of any car, or while in any mail, express, baggage or freight car, or on the locomotive, or while his or her head, limbs or body is projected outside the window or door of any passenger car, in violation of the printed regulations of said corporation posted up at the time in a conspicuous place inside of the passenger cars then in the train, or in violation of any verbal instructions given by any officer of the train, such passenger shall be deemed guilty of contributory negligence, and such corporation shall not be liable for such injury ; *provided*, that there was, at the time, inside of its passenger cars, room sufficient for the accommodation of such passenger.

SEC. 8. Any person who shall in the day or night-time, enter, by force or otherwise, any car of any corporation formed under this act, with intent to steal any valuable thing then and there being, shall be deemed guilty of burglary, and upon conviction thereof shall be punished as in other cases of burglary.

SEC. 9. Any person who shall place any obstruction upon any railroad track of any corporation formed under this act, or displace any switch, or break or remove any rail or tie, or spike, or other thing, or excavate the road-bed or otherwise injure or weaken the same, or cut, or in any other manner interfere with any bridge, or trestle, or culvert, so as to weaken or impair the same, or shall do any other act with intent to throw the cars of such corporation off the track, or to cause a collision between such cars and other cars, or other obstacles or things, shall be deemed guilty of felony ; and upon conviction thereof shall be punished by imprisonment in the state prison for a term not less than five, nor more than ten years ; and, in case such act or acts shall result in injury to the person of another, or shall cause the death of another, such person shall be deemed guilty of an assault with intent to commit murder, or guilty of murder, as the case may be, and upon conviction thereof shall be punished as in other cases of assault with intent to commit murder, and murder.

SEC. 10. It shall be unlawful for any person or persons engaged in mining or other pursuits to tunnel, drift or in any manner excavate under or upon any land belonging to any corporation formed under this act, without the consent of such corporation ; and any person so offending shall be deemed guilty of a misdemeanor ; and on conviction thereof shall forfeit and pay to such corporation treble the amount of damages sustained by reason of such act or acts, and shall be fined not exceeding five hundred dollars, or imprisoned in the county jail not exceeding six months, or shall suffer both such fine and imprisonment in the discretion of the court.

SEC. 11. Any person or persons who shall wilfully do, or cause to be done, any act or acts whatever, whereby any building, construction or work of any kind, or any engine, machine, or structure, or thing, or road-bed, or track, or anything appertaining to such track, or any property belonging to or appertaining to any railroad constructed under this act, or to any corporation formed under this act, shall be weakened, injured, impaired, obstructed, stopped or destroyed, shall be deemed guilty of a misdemeanor, and on conviction thereof shall be fined and imprisoned as provided in the last preceding section of this act, and shall be liable to such corporation for treble the amount of damages which it shall have sustained by reason of such act or acts.

SEC. 12. Every conductor, baggage-master, engineer, brakeman or other employe of any corporation formed under this act, employed on any passenger train, or at stations for passengers, must wear upon his hat or cap, or in some conspicuous place upon the breast of his coat, a badge indicating his office or station, and the initial letters of the name of the corporation by which he is employed. No collector or conductor without such badge shall be authorized to demand or to receive from any passenger any fare, toll or ticket, or exercise any of the powers of his office or station ; and no other officer or employe, without such badge, shall have any authority to meddle or interfere with any passenger or property.

SEC. 13. If any person shall, while in charge of a locomotive engine running upon any railroad of any corporation formed under this act, or while acting as conductor of a car or train of cars on any such railroad, be intoxicated, he shall be deemed guilty of a misdemeanor, and on conviction thereof, shall be fined in any sum not exceeding one thousand dollars, or imprisoned in the county jail not exceeding six months.

SEC. 14. Every corporation formed under this act must provide, and on being tendered the fare therefor, furnish to every person desiring a passage on its cars a ticket which shall entitle the purchaser to a continuous ride and to the accommodations provided on its cars from the station where the same shall be purchased to any other station on the line of its road which the purchaser may designate. The station of departure and the station of destination shall be designated on the face of the ticket.

SEC. 15. Every corporation formed under this act must provide forms of bills of lading in writing, or print and issue any reasonable number thereof to every consignor of freight asking therefor. Said bills of lading must be signed by the agent of such corporation receiving such freight, and must describe the freight so as to identify it and state the name of the consignor and the terms of the contract for carriage. It must also contain an agreement or promise that the freight shall be delivered at the place of destination therein designated to the order or assigns of a particular person or corporation therein designated.

SEC. 16. Any corporation formed under this act shall be exonerated from liability for freight by delivery thereof in good faith to any holder of a bill of lading therefor, properly endorsed or made in favor of the bearer.

SEC. 17. Whenever any corporation has issued a bill of lading for freight, or other instrument substantially equivalent thereto, it may require the surrender thereof, or a reasonable indemnity against claims thereon before delivering the freight therein mentioned.

SEC. 18. Every corporation formed under this act may lawfully demand the payment of fares and freightages in advance; and if they be not paid in advance, such corporation shall have a lien upon the luggage of the passenger for his fare, and upon the freight for freightage due thereon, and may retain possession of such luggage and freight until such fare or freightage shall have been paid. If such fare or freightage be not paid within ten days after the same is due, such luggage or freight may be sold by such corporation in the same manner and with the same consequences as are provided for the sale of unclaimed baggage, in section three of this chapter; *provided*, that if such freight be perishable, it may be sold forthwith at public auction without notice to the owner.

SEC 19. Every corporation formed under this act, within a reasonable time after its road shall have been finally located, must cause a map and profile thereof, and of the land acquired and taken for the use thereof, and the boundaries of the several counties through which the same may run, to be made and file the same in the office of the Secretary of this Territory; and also similar maps of the parts thereof located in different counties, and file the same in the office of the clerk of the county in which such parts of the road shall be situated, there to remain of record forever. In case the line of the road be changed at any time, as in this act provided, similar maps of the new line must be made and filed as aforesaid. Said maps and profiles must be certified by the chief engineer of the corporation, and copies of the same, so filed and certified, must be kept in the office of the secretary of the corporation, subject to examination, by all persons interested, . Copies of such maps and profiles, certified by the Secretary of this Territory, shall be received as *prima facie* evidence of what they contain, in all courts and places within this territory.

SEC. 20. Where the railroad of any corporation formed under this act passes through lands held in private ownership it shall be the duty of such corporation to make and maintain a good and sufficient fence upon each side thereof. In case it does not make and maintain such fence, if its engine or cars shall kill or maim any cattle or other domestic animals belonging to the owner of such land, it shall be liable to such owner for the fair market value of such animal or animals, unless the killing or maiming occurred through the contributory neglect or fault of such owner. If such corporation shall pay to such owner an agreed price for making and maintaining such fence or fences or pay the cost of such fence or fences as part of the damages allowed for right of way through such lands, it shall be relieved and exonerated from all claims for damages arising out of the killing or maiming of any such animals, due, in whole or in part, to the failure of such owner to make and maintain such fences. It shall not be required of such corporation to build such fences until the owner of such land shall have built fences abutting on its road.

SEC. 21. Where the road of any corporation formed under this act passes through lands which, at the time of its construction, were public lands, it shall not be the duty of such corporation to build fences upon either side thereof until after such lands shall have come into private ownership; in which case one-half of such fence or fences shall be built and maintained by such corporation, and the other half by the owner of such lands, unless the latter shall agree for a price to make and maintain the whole. In all other respects, the rights, duties and liabilities of such corporation and owner shall be the same, respectively, as specified in the last preceding section.

SEC. 22. Every corporation formed under this act must make an annual report to the Secretary of this Territory of the operations of the year ending on the 31st of December, which report shall be verified by the president or general superintendent, and the secretary and treasurer of corporation. Such report must be filed in the office of the Secretary of this Territory on or before the first day of March next ensuing, and shall state:

1st. The capital stock, and the amount thereof actually paid in.

2d. The amount paid for the purchase of lands for the construction of the road, for buildings, engines and cars respectively.

3d. The amount and nature of the indebtedness of the corporation, and the amount due to it.

4th. The amount received for the transportation of passengers, property, mails, express matter, respectively, and the amount received from any other sources.

5th. The amount of freight transported, specifying the quantity in tons.

6th. The amount paid for the repair of engines, cars, buildings and other expenses in gross, showing the current expenses of running its road.

7th. The number and amount of dividends, and when paid.

8th. The number of engine-houses and shops, of engines and cars, and their character.

SEC. 23. All railroads constructed under this act may be of such gauge as the board of directors may determine. They must be constructed of the best quality of iron or steel rail, known as " T " or " H " rail, or other pattern of equal utility, until otherwise permitted by law ; *provided*, the provisions of this section shall not apply to railroad tracks used exclusively for carrying freight, or for mining purposes.

SEC. 24. Every corporation formed under this act must commence the construction of its road within two years after the date of the filing of its articles of incorporation in the office of the Secretary of this Territory, and must finish and put the same in full operation within six years thereafter, or its right to further complete the same, in the discretion of the legislative assembly of this Territory, may be forfeited.

[TITLE.]   Chapter IX.

GRANTS, DONATIONS, EXEMPTIONS, DISSOLUTION.

SECTION I. There is hereby granted to every corporation formed under this act a right of way for its railroads and telegraphs to the width of one hundred feet on each side of the center line of the track over and through any of the swamp or overflowed lands or other lands, which now belong to this Territory or may hereafter become the property of this Territory ; and in cases where deep excavations, or heavy embankments, or other cuttings, ditches, drains, canals, culverts or other structures to protect the road-beds and to facilitate the use and enjoyment of the same, is, or may be, required for the grade or other uses of said roads, then, at such places, a greater width of such lands may be taken by such corporation, and the same is hereby further granted to such corporation, not exceeding, in addition, five hundred feet wide. And the right is hereby further granted to such corporation to locate, occupy and hold so much of said lands as may be necessary, for sites and grounds for watering-places, depots, stations or other buildings or structures, along the line of said railroads necessary for the accommodation of the public, the operating of said roads and the transaction of the business of such corporation. And the further right is hereby granted to such corporation to appropriate to its use, by means of pipes, ditches, aqueducts or other conduits so much of the waters of any springs or streams on said lands as may be necessary to the operating of the roads and the transaction of the business of such corporation, together with the right of way over said lands to such springs or streams for such pipes, ditches, aqueducts or other conduits.

SEC. 2. Any county, city or town in this Territory is hereby empowered, by vote of its governing body, to give, grant or donate to any corporation formed under this act the use of any of the streets or highways which may be necessary or convenient to enable such corporation to reach an accessible point for a depot or station in such county, city or town, or to pass through the same on as direct a route as possible so as to accommodate the traveling and commercial interests of such county, city or town.

SEC. 3. To aid and encourage the construction of railroads in this Territory, all the property of every kind and description of every corporation formed under this act shall be exempt from taxation of every kind and description until the expiration of six years from and after the completion of its road or roads ; and the maximum charges for fares and freightages, as fixed by this act shall not be reduced so as to affect any such corporation until the surplus earnings of its roads and tele-, graphs shall exceed ten per cent. upon the cost of the construction and equipment of its roads and telegraphs including the cost of right of way, depots, shops, water rights and stations.

SEC. 4. Any corporation formed under this act may be dissolved by judgment of the District Court for the county in which its principal place of business is situated, upon its voluntary application for that purpose.

SEC. 5. The application must be in writing, and must set forth:

1st. That at a meeting of stockholders called for that purpose, the dissolution of the corporation was resolved upon by a vote representing two-thirds of the subscribed capital stock.

2d. That all claims and demands against the corporation have been satisfied and discharged. The application must be signed by the president and countersigned by the secretary, pursuant to an order of the board of directors entered upon the journal of its proceedings, and sealed with the corporate seal. It must also be verified by the affidavits of the president, secretary and treasurer.

SEC. 6. If the judge be satisfied that the application is in conformity with the provisions of the next preceding section, he must order it to be filed with the clerk of his court, and that such clerk give not less than thirty, nor more than fifty days' notice of the hearing of the application, by publication in some newspaper published in the county, or, if there be no such paper, then by posting such notice in three of the principal public places of the county.

SEC. 7. At any time before the day appointed for hearing the application, any person may file objections, in writing, verified by his oath, to the dissolution of the corporation.

SEC. 8. On the day appointed for the hearing, or on any other day to which the hearing, for any cause, may have been adjourned, the court must proceed to hear and determine the application; and if it shall appear to the satisfaction of the court that all the statements contained in the application are true, it must make a decree declaring such corporation dissolved.

SEC. 9. The application, notice and proof of publication or posting thereof, objections (if any) and the decree of the court shall constitute the judgment roll. An appeal from the judgment may be taken as in other cases.

SEC. 10. Upon the dissolution of the corporation the then directors thereof shall be trustees of the property and assets thereof, for the benefit of creditors and stockholders, and shall have full power to wind up and settle the affairs of the corporation to sell and convey its property, and convert the same into money, and to distribute the same among the stockholders in proportion to the amount of stock held by them, and to that end may use the name of the corporation in all actions and suits, if any such be necessary, to recover and reduce to possession the property, claims, assets and demands of the corporation.

Approved February 2d, 1878.

CHAPTER II.

AN ACT explanatory of an act providing for the incorporation of Railroad Companies in this Territory.

CONTENTS.

Be it enacted by the Legislative Assembly of the Territory of New Mexico:

Section 1. That for the purposes of taxation any railroad or railroads coustructed under the provisions of an act entitled "An act to provide for the incorporation of railroad companies, and the management of the affairs thereof, and other matters relating thereto," approved February 2d, 1878, shall be deemed and are hereby declared to have reached completion, whether at the end of six years from the time of the commencement of the construction thereof, the points to which construction has progressed, and to which said road or roads have been put in operation, is the place of destination of said road or roads as named in the articles of incorporation of the company building or who built the same, or some point intermediate between the termini of said road or roads as named in said articles of incorporation; and that the exemption from taxation for six years from and after the completion of said road or roads, provided for in the above-mentioned act, shall be understood and intended to be exemption from taxation for six years from and after the completion of said road or roads, as such completion is defined and expressed in this act and not otherwise.

And it is hereby expressly provided that in no event shall any line of railway or part of a line railway, or any part or portion of its property, real or personal, privileges, rights or franchises be exempt from taxation for a longer period than twelve years, from and after· the date of the commencement of the construction of such railway or railways.

SEC. 2. This act shall be construed to go along with and as a part of the above-mentioned act, and shall take effect and be in force from and after its passage.

Approved February 15, 1878.

CHAPTER III.

AN ACT in reference to certain Incorporated Companies, in the Territory of New Mexico,

CONTENTS.

Be it enacted by the Legislative Assembly of the Territory of New Mexico :

SECTION 1. That all the powers, privileges and exemptions conferred upon corporations organised under an act entitled an act to provide for the incorporation of railroad companies and the management of the affairs thereof and other matters relating thereto, approved February 2d, A. D. 1878, are hereby conferred upon all corporations incorporated under the laws of this Territory, for the purpose of constructing railroads, and also upon all corporations organized for railroad purposes that have registered in the office of the Secretary of this Territory the original or a certified copy or their articles of incorporation, in accordance with an act entitled an act to amend an act entitled an act to create a general incorporation law, permitting persons to associate themselves together as bodies corporate, for mining, manufacturing and other industrial pursuits, and to repeal the sixteenth section of said act, approved January 30th, 1868.

SEC. 2. That at least one-fourth of the directors of railroad corporations organized under the laws of this Territory shall be residents of this Territory.

SEC. 3. This act shall be in full force and effect from and after its passage and approval.

Approved February 12, 1878.

CHAPTER III.

[AN ACT to amend the General Incorporation Law.

CONTENTS.

Be it enacted by the Legislative Assembly of the Territory of New Mexico:

SECTION 1. Every company or corporation incorporated under the laws of any foreign State or kingdom, or of any State or Territory of the United States, beyond the limits of this Territory, and now or hereafter doing business in this Territory, shall file in the office of the Secretary of this Territory and in the office of the Recorder of Deeds of the county in which the principal place of business of such corporation shall be, a copy of its charter of incorporation, or in case such company is incorporated under any general incorporation law, a copy of its articles of incorporation and of such general incorporation law, all duly certified and authenticated by the proper authority of such foreign State, kingdom or Territory. Such company shall, also, before it is authorized or permitted to do business in this Territory, make and file with the Secretary of the Territory and in the office of the Recorder of Deeds of the county in which its principal place of business shall be, a certificate signed by the president and secretary of such company duly acknowledged, designating the principal place where the business of such company shall be carried on in this Territory, and an authorized agent or agents residing at such principal place of business upon whom process may be served, and such corporations shall have the same powers and shall be subject to all the liabilities and duties as corporations of a like character organized under the general laws of this Territory. But they shall have no other or greater powers, and no foreign or domestic corporation established or maintained in any way for pecuniary profit of its stockholders or members, shall purchase or hold real estate in this Territory except as provided for in this act and the laws of the Territory now existing, and no corporation doing business in this Territory, incorporated under the laws of any other State, shall be permitted to mortgage, pledge or otherwise encumber its real or personal property, situated in this Territory, to the injury or exclusion of any citizen, citizens or corporations of this Territory who are creditors of such foriegn corporation, and no mortgage by any foreign corporation, except railroad and telegraph companies, given to secure any debt created in any other State, shall take effect as against any citizen or corporation of this Territory until all its liabilities due to any person or corporation in this Territory at the time of recording such mortgage have been paid and extinguished.

SEC. 2. A failure to comply with the provisions of the foregoing section shall render each and every officer, agent and stockholder of any such corporation so failing, jointly, severally and personally liable on any and all contracts of such company made within this Territory during the time that such company is so in default.

SEC. 3. The several certificates, charters and statutes mentioned in section one of this act shall be by the Secretary of the Territory, filed and preserved in his office, and he shall be entitled therefor to the same fees as are allowed him by law for filing articles of incorporation. Copies of such charters, statutes and certificates, duly certified by the Secretary of the Territory under his seal of office, shall be competent evidence in all courts of this Territory of the corporate character of such companies and of their powers, duties and liabilities, and the originals thereof may be used in like manner, be used in evidence of these matters with like effect.

SEC. 4. Suits may be instituted and prosecuted by and against any corporation formed or recognized (organized) under this act in the same manner and in like cases as natural persons.

SEC. 5. The certified copy of any articles of incorporation and changes thereof, together with all endorsements therein (thereon,) under the great seal of the Territory of New Mexico, shall be taken and received in all courts and places as *prima facie* evidence of the facts therein stated.

SEC. 6. In suits against any corporation summons shall be served in that county where the principal office of the corporation is kept or its principal business carried on, by delivering a copy to the president thereof, it he may be found in said county, but if he is absent there-from, then the summons shall be served in like manner in [the] county on either the vice-president, secretary, treasurer, cashier, general agent, general superintendent or stockholder, or any agent of said corporation, within such time and under such rules as are provided by law for the service of such process in suits against real persons, and if no such person can be found in the county where the principal office of the corporation is kept, or in the county where its principal business is carried on, to serve such process upon, a summons may issue from either one of such counties, directed to the sheriff of any county in this Territory where any such person may be found and served with process. If such corporation keeps no principal office in any county, and there is no county in which the principal business of such corporation is carried on, then suit may be brought against it in any county where the above-mentioned officers, or any or either of them may be found; provided, that the plaintiff may, in all cases. bring his action in the county where the cause of action accrued.

SEC. 7. It shall be the duty of the directors or trustees of every such corporation, except railroad or telegraph corporations, to cause a book to be kept by the secretary or clerk thereof containing the names of all persons, alphabetically arranged, who are or shall, within one year, have been stockholders of such corporation, and showing their places of residence, the number of shares of stock held by them respectively, and the time when they respectively became the owners of such shares, and the time when they ceased to be such stockholders, and the amount of stock actually paid in, and what proportion has been paid in cash; which book shall, during the usual business hours of the day be open for the inspection of the stockholders and creditors of the company and their personal representatives, at the office or principal place of business of such company in the county where its business operations shall be located; and any and every such stockholders, creditors or representative shall have a right to make extracts from such books, and no transfer of stock shall be valid for any purpose whatever, except to render the person to whom it shall be transferred liable for the debts of the company, according to the provisions of this act. unless it shall have [been] entered therein as required by this section, within sixty days from the date of such transfer, by an entry showing to and from whom transferred. Such books shall be presumptive evidence of the facts therein stated in any suit or proceedings of such corporation, or against any one or more stockholders. Every officer or agent of any such company who shall neglect to make any proper entry in such book, or shall refuse or neglect to exhibit the same or allow the same to be inspected and extracts taken therefrom, shall be, as provided by this section, deemed guilty of a misdemeanor, and the corporation shall forfeit and pay to the party injured a penalty of fifty dollars for every such neglect or refusal and all the damages resulting therefrom.

SEC. 8. The dissolution for any cause whatever of corporations created as aforesaid, shall not take away or impair any remedy given against such corporations, its stockholders or officers for any liabilities incurred previous to its dissolution.

SEC. 9. Corporations may be formed and may do business in this Territory under the laws of the Territory now existing, and subject to the provisions of this act, to acquire, hold, improve, develop and manage any hot, mineral or other sanitary spring, or to lay off land into town sites, blocks, lots, streets, alleys, avenues, commons and parks, and to acquire, hold, colonize, improve and sell lands in connection with any or all of said objects.

SEC. 10. This act shall be in force from and after its passage, and all laws in conflict herewith are repealed.

Approved February 12, 1880.

CHAPTER IV.

AN ACT in Relation to Railroad Corporations.

CONTENTS.

Section 1. Must elect, under which law, proceedings in condemnation of property shall be had.

Be it enacted by the Legislative Assembly of the Territory of New Mexico:

SECTION 1. That in all proceedings for the condemnation of lands, timber, stone, gravel, water or other materials for the uses and purposes of any railroad corporations, organized and existing under the laws of this Territory, such railroad corporation shall be and hereby is required to elect under which of the several acts now in force it desires to effect such condemnation, which election shall be set out in the application for condemnation, and when such election is made proceedings shall be had under and according to the provisions of the act such corpora- . tion may elect to proceed under.

SEC. 2. That all acts and parts of acts in conflict with this act are hereby repealed, and this act shall take effect and be in force from and after its passage.

Approved February 13, 1880.

www.ingramcontent.com/pod-product-compliance
Lightning Source LLC
Chambersburg PA
CBHW021628270326
41931CB00008B/917